STORI'
FROM
THE SHOP

A 1950s childhood

Geraldine Outhwaite

CHURNET VALLEY BOOKS
Leek, Staffordshire. ST13 5NW 01538 399033
www.leekbooks.co.uk
© Geraldine Outhwaite and Churnet Valley Books 2012 ISBN 9781904546863

Especially to my Mum, Dad and Mamma, with love.
And all the relations and friends mentioned in the book.

'The past is a foreign country, they do things differently there.'
L P Hartley

Contents

Chapter 1:   Taking Tizer with the Booths   p. 6

Chapter 2:   Eddie Breadie and the Yates   p. 11

Chapter 3:   Stafford, the Dansette and Little Richard   p. 15

Chapter 4:   The Bus to Biddulph Moor   p. 18

Chapter 5:   Florrie Bailey's Corner Shop   p. 24

Chapter 6:   Visiting Billy Booth's Workshop   p. 27

Chapter 7:   The Relentless Rain
                      and the Macclesfield Step   p. 31

Chapter 8:   Grammy's Wednesday Visits   p. 36

Chapter 9:   Mary Ellen Doorbar née Whalley   p. 41

Chapter 10: Being A Bridesmaid   p. 52

Chapter 11: Bonfire Night at Auntie Al's   p. 58

Chapter 12: Uncle George's Bubble Car   p. 59

Chapter 13: Stories from the Scotia Road Shop   p. 66

Chapter 14: The Holiday Caravan
                      - from Talacre to Longsdon   p. 72

Chapter 15: Brownhills, Shakespeare
                      and the Snow of '63   p. 79

Chapter 16: Christmas, the Front Bedroom
                      and the Victorian Ghost   p. 93

Myself, taken in the front room of 67 Park Lane Knypersley, in the mid 1950s with my much loved part-Persian ginger cat.

Mamma, Mary Ellen Doorbar in her early 50s, taken on holiday.

Preface

This is an episodic telling of the story of my life growing up in the Staffordshire Moorlands in the 1950s and early 1960s. The stories start with and are simply told from the point of view of a young 7 year old child, ranging through to my school life when I was 12 years of age. The common theme running through the stories is the backdrop of my family's various small shops which they kept. It was after all still the age of the small shopkeeper. It is also the time when extended families lived closer together and certainly grandmothers, great grandmothers, aunties, uncles, great aunts and uncles and cousins all played a big part in my growing up just like my mother and father. I was blanketed in care by my relatives and although an only child never felt like one. Just like in the tales of Milly Molly Mandy by Joyce Lankester Brisley I was a child growing up with lots of adult companionship.

There were a lot of joys in my 1950s childhood. Everyone who grew up in the 1950s in Britain will have his or her own indelible memories of their childhood, from their first taste of welfare orange juice to the birth of rock 'n 'roll. The nation was recovering from the ravages of the Second World War and the camaraderie of wartime was still evident throughout the country. As a child I felt free to explore my surroundings and not fearful about doing so.

To illustrate the stories I have included personal photographs of the people, places, products and artefacts of the times to evoke the spirit of times past. I hope you enjoy the telling of one childhood relived. If you are of a similar age to me, please compare your growing up to my own and enjoy and marvel at the differences and similarities.

Geraldine Outhwaite
Harriseahead
Stoke-on-Trent
Staffs ST7 4JT

All the drawings are by the author except those on pages 2 and 93.

Myself as a small child in about 1953/54 in the front garden of 65 Park Lane, which was next door to the bungalow shop which my Mamma, Mary Ellen Doorbar ran. In the centre background you can see the cottage where Mr and Mrs Booth lived.

My mother and father, Thelma Doorbar and Harry Berrisford as a young couple in the late 1940s.

The bungalow 67 Park Lane Knypersley, in the 1950s, where my mum, dad and I lived - this was 2 doors away from the shop.

1. Taking Tizer at the Booths

In the 1950s my grandmother, Mary Doorbar ran a small grocery/general shop from the front of her bungalow on Park Lane, Knypersley. (It is still there by the way and is once again trading as a grocery shop.) The siting of the shop meant that it had many potential customers. Firstly there were the householders on Park Lane itself which ran the length from Knypersley crossroads to virtually Rock End. It was also close to the nearby miners' estate of council housing which led off from Woodland Street. My grandmother's shop was also on the bend in the road opposite Conway Road where Harry Jones, the builder had begun building his estate of privately owned, detached and semi-detached bungalows. The estate had street names all with a Welsh connection e.g. Harlech Drive, Menai Drive. Her shop was therefore a thriving small business.

As a toddler, I was used to toddling into the shop and peering over the counter to 'eye' the customers. As I got older, I was able to stack the shelves with tinned goods (good for hand and eye co-ordination in children) and when a little older still I was able to take a few orders out to local elderly customers who appreciated this 'service'.

One couple I used to deliver small items to was an elderly couple, in their 80s, called Mr and Mrs Booth. Some years later I was to realise this couple was related to my best friend at Biddulph Moor Primary School, Margaret Booth, the youngest daughter of Billy Booth, the undertaker, but alas at the time I didn't put such facts together. The elderly Mr Booth was a retired joiner, who had helped in the undertaking business and his wife had been a very good dressmaker. She had made a beautiful suit for my Auntie Betty. They had retired to Knypersley for an easier, (warmer probably), less-isolated, way of life.

I only had to cross the road from the shop to their bungalow, with such deliveries as a bottle of milk and a loaf of bread but I did find my visits memorable if brief. I would arrive outside their lean-to conservatory which was connected to the side of their white-washed bungalow and knock on the door. I remember it always seemed to be full of scarlet, pink, showy flowering geraniums, whatever the weather, and when Mr Booth appeared at the door and led me through the conservatory; it was warm and smelt of the earth and sunshine.

Often, Mr Booth had a clutch of speckled eggs in his brown, knotty fingers and his eyes would twinkle as he asked 'Do you want to see the chicks?' I would always want to see the chicks, so he led me through the conservatory and into the backyard where his hen shed was. We would go into the shed and on a large bread tray, often with a strong lamp overhead for the warmth; I'd find tens of teeny, fluffy, yellow chicks cheeping away as they tottered about and over one another in their bid to get used to the world and their environment. Suitably enthralled for moments, we would just concentrate on watching them and being amused by their newness and unsteadiness. Mr Booth, grey-whiskered and bedecked with his chequered cloth cap (at all times, it seemed) would smile at me and them, then after a suitable time of watching had gone by, would lead me back into the back kitchen of the house where I would deposit the bread and milk on the wooden kitchen table.

Mrs Booth would enter and usher me through from the kitchen into the front, wood-lined, dark parlour where I would sit to drink my reward for this errand, a glass of Tizer. I had to wait for the reward while Mrs Booth returned to the kitchen to prepare it. I would sit rigidly in my chintzy armchair, hardly daring to breathe and move, whilst Mrs Booth padded quietly around the kitchen accompanied by soft tinklings. I sat listening to the slow, deep tick-tock of the walled grandfather clock and sniffing the oily, pungent smell of the freshly-polished furniture. The room was stuffed so full of old-fashioned heavy furniture that it seemed to fit into the room like pieces of a jigsaw. I know it was always

An advertisement sign of the time, promoting the popular soft drink. Tizer.

difficult to make my way to the comfy, roomy armchair. How the elderly couple moved around the room with ease, I will never know.

At last the crystal glass with its fizzing, orange, popping liquid would arrive on a small, round tray. Mrs Booth would set it next to me, on the be-tasselled, velvet maroon cloth which covered the huge round, dining table. She would sit down with me good-naturedly, in companionable silence while I drank my Tizer. This privileged front room visit lasted only minutes once the pop was drunk, as I was then swiftly up and daintily picking my path through the furniture-laden room, back to the kitchen and the door, by which I had come in. Mr Booth, with his twinkly, crinkly eye-slits stood at the door as I rendered my relieved 'goodbye.' Relieved, only because, I feared breaking something in the front room visit, with its packed furniture, and delicate treasures on display.

I remember that I always looked forward to my next grocery delivery there and the reward for my small courtesy. I must have been 9 or 10 when I delivered the groceries. I had moved on to secondary school and a different local area when Mr and Mrs Booth were no longer in need of a grocery delivery. The memory of their quiet gentleness and good-nature has stayed with me.

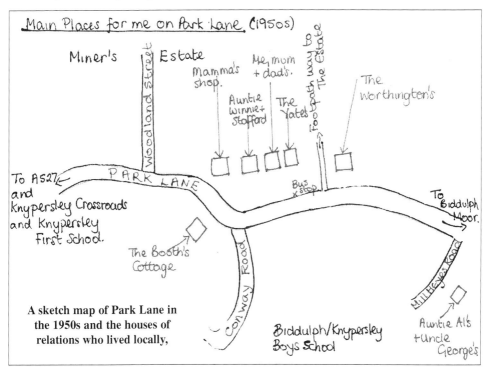

A sketch map of Park Lane in the 1950s and the houses of relations who lived locally,

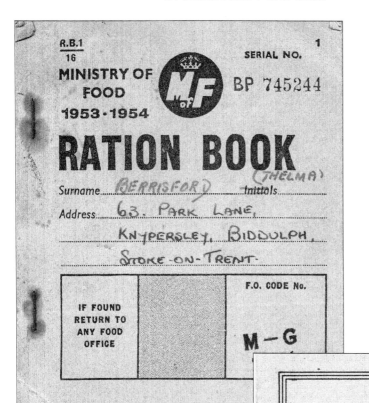

The front of my mother's ration book.
She worked in the Food Office in Biddulph
as a young woman and issued the books.
Rationing didn't end completely until 1954.

My identity card when I was a young child.

2. Eddie Breadie and the Yates

In the 1950s my grandmother (Mamma), Mary Doorbar, ran a small grocery/ general shop from the front of her bungalow on Park Lane, Knypersley. The shop was a specially fitted store not just a converted front room or shed as some small shops were at that time. At the front was a sizeable yard where delivery vans or customers' cars could park. Most customers did come to shop on foot. On Friday evenings my dad would also deliver a number of orders by car in cardboard boxes to valued customers, so saving them a journey to collect a heavy load of goods. (Just as an aside, I looked up the cost of a gallon of petrol in 1956 and found the figure '2 gallons of Esso petrol was 9 shillings and 4 old pence.' That is of course just under 50p in today's currency.)

Me, outside the family car, my dad inside it. The car not only ferried us about but was used as a delivery vehicle taking orders out to customers surrounding the bungalow shop on Park Lane.

The shop had a large plate-glass window that you could look through and see inside and view the stock before going in. Inside, I remember it had an L-shape arrangement of counters. One was a waist-high glass-topped unit with shelves in it to display cakes and edible goods like bacon and ham; any produce in fact that was unwrapped and needed to be protected against dust and flies. I remember the counter was finished in chromium edging that in the summer was cool and smooth to the touch. There were shelves on two sides of the walls behind the counters which displayed tinned goods, soap powders, vinegars, tea, and coffee - in fact all the usual daily items that a housewife would require. Cheese was cut with a wire cutter on a board to the required weight or dimensions the customer wanted. Two cheeses were on offer, either white Cheshire or yellow Cheddar. On the other side of the counter fresh vegetables were kept on the floor and could be weighed out by the customer themselves. Again the choice was limited to potatoes, carrots, and onions with possible seasonal changes adding to the range.

When I got to about 7, I used to particularly enjoy the visits of the delivery men that came to the shop. There were quite a few of them that came, with bread, milk, fruit and fresh vegetables. One step up from the delivery men were the 'travellers' as my grandmother used to refer to them. These were men often smarter, carrying sample cases and dressed in dark suits, rather than aprons or overalls, who were commercial travelling salesmen. They came to try and persuade my grandmother to stock new lines or brands of stock. This was not an easy job as my grandmother was an astute business woman and knew just what her customers would buy.

However to return to the delivery men. One such delivery man was Eddie Breadie. I don't know what his real name was but I named him that because of the goods he delivered. He came to deliver the daily order of bread, I can't remember if he was the Embrey's or the Mother's Pride man, (both brands made locally) but what I do remember is that after he had brought in the bread on the large wire trays, I would somehow wangle a lift in his van up to my mum and dad's bungalow, all of two bungalows away. I would get into the front seat of his van with him, no seat belts then (and definitely against Health and Safety regulations now) and enjoy the short, swift ride to my house. Eddie Breadie was a cheerful young man with brylcreemed, neat black hair and a black moustache, who also seemed to enjoy this small taxi service which he ran for me. Sometimes my next door neighbour and friend, Alan Yates, would also be given the lift with me, (if he was about at the time.) Both of us would then cram into the small front seat of the cream, delivery van and get the lift to our bungalows. This lift became a regular feature of our routine and somehow this small act delighted and enriched our young lives.

Often we would both go and play in Alan's garden, which was a long rectangle of scruffy grass at the back of the Yates' bungalow. Alan was the youngest of the Yates' children and my age. (He had an older brother and sister, Brian and Margaret.) We would start off playing around the back door within sight of Alan's mum, Mrs Yates (or Irene as my Mamma called her). Mrs Yates was a jolly, cheerful woman who was often singing. You could hear her singing from our back garden or hear her infectious laughter, which again echoed around to our back garden. (Her happiness was more remarkable, I deduced, when over hearing a conversation amongst the adults, because 'she was not a well woman').

Alan and I would play with a ball or at just being silly, it didn't seem to take much to amuse us as children. Well, we would play until our silliness got too rowdy and Mr Yates would yell from the back bedroom to tell us to 'go and play somewhere else.' He was a miner and shift worker so would be sleeping in the day, and understandably got annoyed when his sleep was disturbed. That was our cue then, to go and play in my garden.

We would go off giggling as quietly as we could - suppressing the giggles often made us snort with laughter even more - squash ourselves through a gap in the dividing privet hedging (no point in walking all the way around to the gate, if you didn't have to) and resume our playing in my garden. Alan had a particular, distinctive, infectious laugh. It was loud, at squeal pitch, like the whinny of a young, lively, excitable colt and continued until you could not help but join in.

I remember some of the ways that we used to pass the time. It was riding bikes, or skating, pogo-sticking (that was not a cruel sport, but just jumping about on a pogo stick, well mine anyway.) You could make your own stilts by getting two oblong chunks of wood and wrapping long pieces of string around them. Then you could

My mother, father and mamma, taken under the apple trees in the back garden of 67 Park Lane, Knypersley.

put your feet on the wood blocks underneath the string, pull tightly on the pieces of string and propel yourself along the ground. This was not an easy game option because after a few parades around the back yard a) you had to be careful that the string didn't cut off the circulation to your feet and b) you were quite worn out! We might also spend time watching my dad's few hens that were fenced off and scratching away under the apple trees in the back garden. Occasionally we would throw things over our back garden fence into the field at the back (not exactly a mind-stretching activity.)

We would run all the way around our bungalow playing 'tick.' I remember during one energetic running game, I was not looking where I was going, managed to fall after tripping down a grid hole and broke my wrist. The doctor at the Haywood Hospital, where it was set called it a 'greenstick fracture'. For the shock, my Mamma gave me a very small amount of whiskey in water (before going to the hospital to have it set.) That was going to some lengths to have my first taste of alcohol!

If we got really fed-up and it was the long summer holiday, we would take ourselves across the road and into the farmer's fields that took up the area around Conway Road. The bungalows that Harry Jones built were in the process of being built then, but there was still, in the summer, acres of golden wheat fields that you could play in. We made paths and runs in the ripening wheat, I remember, trampling it down. We fell down laughing until we coughed through exhaustion from running. I never remember being told off by anyone about harming the crops.

People often describe the 1950s now as being boring and bland and monochrome and perhaps they were but I also remember being very happy and safe as a child and having a lot of freedom and room to grow up and just 'be a child' in. The 1950s were idyllic to me.

3. Stafford, the Dansette and Little Richard

In the 1950s your relatives and extended family lived closer to one another. For instance, in the bungalow next to my grandmother's shop there lived one of her sisters and her son. My great aunt helped my grandmother in the shop, both were widows so they needed to make a living. Next to their bungalow we lived - my mum, dad and me. I remember nipping between the three bungalows and going into them all at will, whenever I liked. Higher up Park Lane, going towards Biddulph Moor, my aunty's mother and father, Mr and Mrs Worthington, lived. Higher up still and a short bike ride for me, along

Great Auntie Winnie, my Mamma and Grammy with Stafford, taken in the late 1940s.

Mill Heyes Road, my dad's sister Aunty Alice and her husband had a bungalow. And that was all in a half mile range.

So I grew up thinking that you always knew the people you lived alongside and that they were related to you! Just like Milly Molly Mandy in the Joyce Lankester Brisley stories, I was a little girl growing up surrounded by a lot of adult relatives. I could draw a similar map to the one drawn in the front of the Milly Molly Mandy books showing her village, except mine would illustrate Park Lane homes and the people who lived in them. Contrast this social and family arrangement with that of today, with increased individual and family mobility, often couples are bringing up their children in isolation without the support of an extended family and the advantages that can bring.

To return to my story however. My great aunt and her son, who was ten years older than me, were great companions. I was impressed by the experiences and life of my older 'great' cousin. For a start, he got about on a scooter, which was very 'mod' for Knypersley in the later 1950s. He not only travelled to work on it but obviously used it for his own amusement and to take excursions on.

I remember that he was very fond of American popular music and he had at one stage a fanaticism for the American singer Little Richard (or Little Dickie as another great uncle preferred to call him). An enlarged picture of the popstar's face with his iconic, combed-back dark quiff and pencil line moustache was sellotaped onto the inside of the lid of his green Dansette record player and at various intervals during the weekend, gales of guitar riffs and choruses of 'Good Golly Miss Molly' would twang and blare through the back door. Often I would go around to the house and have a bop to manic piano playing and raspy shouted vocals as both Little Richard and my cousin sang 'Tutti Frutti' and 'Long Tall Sally'. This exciting rock and roll was a far cry from the sedateness of 1950s life in Knypersley and my grandmother's favourite music, Mantovani and his stringed orchestra.

Amazingly Little Richard came to play in the UK (before his conversion to Christianity) in the 1950/60s; he came to play at Trentham Gardens, I believe. Naturally, Stafford had to go but who would go with him? Who shared his passion for Little Richard and his music? Not many people that he knew did. Who were the people most likely to enjoy such a concert and could share the excitement of a rock and roll performance? Who could go?

Well naturally the choice was his mother and his aunt (my grandmother.) Both quite sedate ladies and in their fifties themselves at the time. I don't know how the three got there but go to the concert they did. I believe as well that some of the audience were sitting at tables during the evening and towards the end of it, trouble broke out amongst the fans. I can only imagine the picture of two middle aged ladies, with their sensible coats, matching hats and capacious, matching handbags in the audience of a Little Richard concert especially when it got rowdy. Needless to say the 'slight unplibrium. I think they enjoyed the unexpected experience and certainly Stafford has to be commended for taking two such companions to the concert without a zintilla of embarrassment.

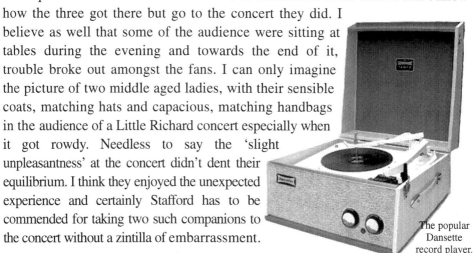

The popular Dansette record player.

A poster of the time for Trentham Gardens.

Inset, a picture of Little Richard in the 1950s.

TRENTHAM GARDENS

THE BEAUTY SPOT
OF THE MIDLANDS

- GARDENS AND MILE LONG LAKE
- MOTOR LAUNCHES AND ROWING BOATS
- MINIATURE RAILWAY TRIPS
- OPEN AIR SWIMMING POOL
- LARGEST BALLROOM IN MIDLANDS
- BOWLS, PUTTING, TENNIS ETC.
- CHILDREN'S PLAYGROUND
- AMPLE PARKING SPACE FOR CARS & MOTOR COACHES
- ADMISSION TO GARDENS ADULTS 1/6 CHILDREN 9ᵈ

3 miles from
STOKE-ON-TRENT
on the main
LONDON
MANCHESTER
ROAD

ENQUIRIES TO –
CATERING MANAGER
TRENTHAM GARDENS LTD
THE BALLROOM
TRENTHAM
NEAR STOKE-ON-TRENT
TELEPHONE TRENTHAM

LUNCHEONS
TEAS
AT MODERATE PRICES
LARGE AND SMALL PARTIES
CATERED FOR

EXCELLENT BUS SERVICE TO
THE GARDENS ENTRANCE

A PMT (Potteries Motor Traction) bus of the 1950s.

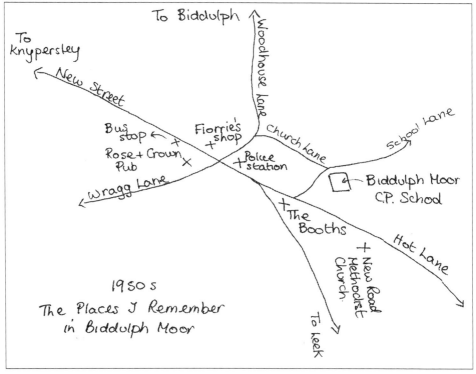

To Biddulph

To Knypersley

← New Street

Woodhouse Lane

Bus stop ←   ✕

Fiorrie's
+ shop

Church Lane

School Lane

Rose + Crown
Pub   ✕

+ Police
station

Wragg Lane ←

⬜ ← Biddulph Moor
C.P. School

+ The
Booths

Hot Lane

+ New Road
Methodist
Church

1950s
The Places I Remember
in Biddulph Moor

To Leek

4. The Bus to Biddulph Moor

Unlike the rest of the children who lived on Park Lane, Alan (my next door neighbour and friend) and I went to Biddulph Moor County Primary School. The first school at the bottom of the road at Knypersley crossroads was nearer but Alan and I caught the red PMT bus every morning, which would stop just outside Alan's front gate. The bus ride must have lasted 10 minutes at the most but it was an enjoyable and a different way to start our day.

Why I went to this school in preference to the nearer local Knypersley School, I'm not quite sure. I do know that the headmaster there, Mr Holmes, had been the headmaster at my dad's school and he (my dad) must have thought him good enough to teach his daughter. Mr Smith Holmes was a lovely, fatherly, cultured man. He must have been in his middle years, tall and well-built. He had thinning, balding hair with a genial smile always. I remember he often wore a greenish suit to school. He also had a beautifully named daughter, Isabel. On odd occasions Isabel would come into our school with her father and it was always a special occasion if Isabel was coming. Her name alone conjured up a romantic, idealistic young girl, an image which the real Isabel did not shatter.

But back to the school bus ride. All my school career at Biddulph Moor, the

A recent picture of Biddulph Moor County Primary School now called Moor First School. Not a great deal has changed in this view, although the windows, school sign and lamp-post are new.

conductor on the bus was a young man called Charlie Lancaster (he hardly seemed to take a day off). He had black, brylcreemed-back hair and a pencil thin black moustache. (It must have been a trend at the time, the thin 'tache a la Clarke Gable, as there were a lot of them about.) He wore a dark blue/black uniform with a matching peaked cap, and dispensed tickets from his ticket machine with confidence. He lurched up and down the bus aisle, dispensing tickets as the bus ground its way up and down the hills to Biddulph Moor.

Charlie was a very easy-going young man, as I remember often there were high-spirited journeys back from school which consisted of a lot of seat swapping and general movement. I was also in the habit of doing 'tipple-overs' between the seats in the bus aisle as it moved along! All behaviour of course would not be tolerated today from the Health and Safety angle or indeed by the lone driver operating the buses today.

Journeys in the winter months could often in the 1950s be halted by heavy snowfalls. Then the narrow lanes around the Moor were blocked and cut off by five, six or seven feet snowdrifts. If these occurred we didn't go to school. Temperatures were often very low, below freezing. I remember frequently seeing perfectly-formed dagger-like, crystal icicles of all sizes ranged along the spouting on the outside of houses and the school. They could be a foot long or more. The outside school toilets often froze. (The school did not get inside flush toilets until about 1962 after I left.) The free third of a pint of milk we received, was often served with a milk popsicle rising up from the lid where the milk had frozen and expanded. Comically the foil lid would be still attached to the top of the popsicle like a small hat.

But Christmases, despite the cold, were lovely at Biddulph Moor. We had a carol concert naturally. We made Christmas cards and calendars to take home to our families. One year mine consisted of an embroidered Mother Christmas in bright, red corduroy with cotton wool trimmings and the year date stub attached to it. We had a Christmas dinner and a lovely party afterwards. I am not sure now who used to dress up as Santa Claus, but of course Santa came and handed out an individual present to each child. I still have two of my Christmas presents which have survived intact - a Wade model of PC Plod (from the Noddy

books) and a Wade model of Lady out of Disney's 'Lady and the Tramp.' There was the excitement of going up to Santa and collecting your present. Mr Holmes made Christmas magical for all the children at his school.

At the end of some glacial school days, we were glad to get on the bus and return home. Although since these were the pre-central heating days in private homes, unless you sat directly in front of the open coal fire, you were cold for most of the winter even indoors. I would sit inches from and ages in front of the blazing kitchen fire in winter until the front of my legs were red mottled toasted lumps, whilst the back of my legs were still milk-pale and cold. The height of luxury for me was when my grandmother had spread-eagled my vest and liberty bodice over the metal fire guard on winter mornings, so that I could dress in an underwear layer of toasting hot clothes in front of a molten-hot fire before I went out to school.

Summer was a different matter however. Often on warm summer days after school, I wouldn't catch the bus back home at all but would run, skip and walk there. I'd enjoy passing through all the smaller areas that made up my journey. Walking along past the cottages on New Street where my mum and dad's friends Handel and Vera Bailey lived; climbing up the hill to Robin Hill and then onward past the farm where the Harvey brothers lived. Onwards to Rock End and to the sharp right hand bend which began the slow descent to Park Lane, passing Lodge Barn Road and Bailey's farm on the left. I know I would often then arrive home after my exertions complaining that I had a stitch in my left side! No wonder, when I'd virtually run the two or so miles back home.

Summer terms at the school were idyllic. I can remember nature walks and sitting in sunshine-lit fields amongst bluey harebells, pale pink lady's smock, chimney sweeps, and tall meadow buttercups like miniature candelabras. And you always had to play the 'Do you like butter game?' with the flower heads by holding them directly under your friend's chin to see if they glowed yellow. We played games of cricket in the school yard (no discrimination here, the girls played as well as the boys) and rounders.

One summer, during the roller skate craze, all the girls took their roller skates to school. In the roomy schoolyard, we would all hold hands in a long line and skate around in a large circle. Of course we would take turns to be the child on the end of the line who was whipped around at such a velocity that it was half expected you might launch into orbit, given a fair wind. The lads would also helpfully lay down in the yard and act as obstacles for us to challengingly skate

Geraldine Beresford

Staffordshire Education Committee.

BIDDULPH MOOR COUNTY PRIMARY SCHOOL.

Report for Term Ending ..... *April 8th 1960.* ......

Class....*2*..... No in class...*35*... Position in class.............

Arithmetic.		out of	
Tables.			*Good*
Mental.			*Good*
Mechanical.	*33*	*45*	*Good*
Problems.			
English.			*Good*
Spelling.			*✓ Good*
Writing.			*A neat and careful worker.*
Composition.			
Reading.	*11*	*12.*	*V. Good.*
Geography.			
History.			
Nature.			
Handwork. Needlework.			
Art.			*Has produced some pleasing results.*

General Remarks. *Geraldine was absent for most of the tests so there is no class position.*
Her work throughout the year has been of a high standard. She is a consistently neat and careful worker.

Well done !

J. Beresford

Class Teacher. *N. Cooper.* ....

Head Teacher. *M. Holmes* ....

around. This exercise was designed to improve our skating skills. (We found out later that they were actually using the opportunity to look up our skirts! Well, we put an end to that game naturally.) We played hopscotch in the school playground and had some climbing bars to use. However we had no springy, rubbery playmates to land on then, just the tarmac of the yard. Knees were constantly grazed and covered with strategically.applied plasters

To start at the beginning though, Biddulph Moor School, (as I knew it) was built by the council in 1908 because of growing numbers of children and the overcrowding of the original school at Christ Church Hall. The original school was built by public subscription in 1852 and with the aid of James Bateman of the Grange. Later additions were funded by Robert Heath, also later of the Grange. During WW2 part of it was used by the War Office and during that time the infants joined the 'top school' from Christ Church Hall. As 'top school' infers it was only the junior intake that at first used the council built new school.

When I went to the school both infants and juniors attended. There were four teachers there and four classes with about 100 children attending. Mrs Warrender taught the infants and reception class. Mrs Brookes, a local farmer's wife, ran the next class. Both these classes were at the same end of the school to the right of Mr Holmes' office. At the other end of the school, Mr Cooper (the son of another headmaster) ran the first juniors, and the top juniors were Mr Holmes' own class. We learned poetry with Mr Holmes eg Browning's 'Home Thoughts from Abroad', and mental arithmetic - we chanted our times tables together. We also did music with Mr Holmes, he was an accomplished pianist and in school assemblies would play us into the hall/dining room with his version of 'Moonlight Sonata'.

It was Mr Holmes who suggested to my mum and dad that I have singing and music lessons because he thought that I had a good voice and was musical. They took his advice and I did have lessons which continued for the next seven years of my life. I was a very happy child growing up in the school which he ran and was one of the schoolchildren that passed their 11+ in the 1960s, with his guidance, which enabled me to go onto Brownhills, the all girls' grammar school in Stoke-on-Trent. From there, I went on to study at University. Not a bad result for a pupil from a small county primary school in the Staffordshire Moorlands.

OPPOSITE PAGE:
My School report from 1960, signed by my class teacher Mr Cooper and countersigned by Mr Holmes. Unfortunately, I missed a lot of tests through illness that year when I had a bout of whooping cough.

5. Florrie Bailey's Corner Shop

Most days as an after school treat, I would call (along with the rest of the school, it seemed) at Florrie's on New Street. Her small, corner shop was only a coal shed-sized hut but behind the counter were shelves of countless, filled clear glass sweet bottles. They seemed to be arranged in disciplined rows like waiting soldiers with red-topped lids, guarding their individual confectionery contents.

The bottles held cheery miniature cherry lips which were 2 or 3d for a triangular, white paper bag full. There were yellow sherbet dip-dabs with a liquorice wand to dip with or you could buy the loose sherbet,which looked like multi-coloured, swirling, sand grains, from a bottle on display. We could buy 4 chewy blackjacks for 1d or traffic light gobstoppers which changed colour as you sucked them. There were maroon, delicious aniseed balls of ball-bearing proportions that you sucked until they turned white and dissolved.

My favourite of favourites were the multi-coloured liquorice comfits that had a hard candy coat, which you had to crunch before you got to the liquorice kernel. I picked out the scarlet ones first, licked them, then applied them as lipstick. These were just some of my favourites! Whatever you bought, they would sustain you on the journey back home.

You remember also that my own grandmother owned a general grocery shop, so what I was doing buying goods from a competitor I really do not know. I suppose Florrie was not really close enough to be such and it was a treat to come straight out of school and buy my own sweets. Being from a shop, I was quite a connoisseur of sweets and toffees on sale at that time. I know I had my own classifications for sweets, some of which went as follows.

Lucky bags - good value and worth it to get the surprise gift
Flying saucers - made of a thin wafer and sherbet that stuck to the roof of your mouth unsettlingly
Sherbet Fountains - always worth getting
Gob stoppers - have to give your full attention to sucking these; because if you spoke or laughed there was a danger that they would shoot towards your throat and choke you
Aniseed balls - a favourite
Imps - so strong you have to breathe in through your mouth noticeably to cool the inside of your mouth down

Zubes - I like the white powder that they are dusted with
Sky-ray lollies - if you didn't eat them quickly in the summer, you got multi-coloured stickiness dripping down all over your hand from the melting lolly. This was very uncomfortable.
Fruit gums - had a tendency to get stuck in between your teeth, so you had to do a bit of finger-jiggling with them to release them
Fruit pastilles -good
Milky Way - one of my favourite chocolate bars because it was so smooth and easy to eat
Mars bars - too much and too sickly for me to eat at one go
Juicy fruit gum - good
Cola cubes/Pineapple chunks - have a tendency to make the roof of my mouth sore, so don't eat
Cadbury's Five Boys bar - had the heads of five boys impressed on it, which I particularly enjoyed nibbling away at first.

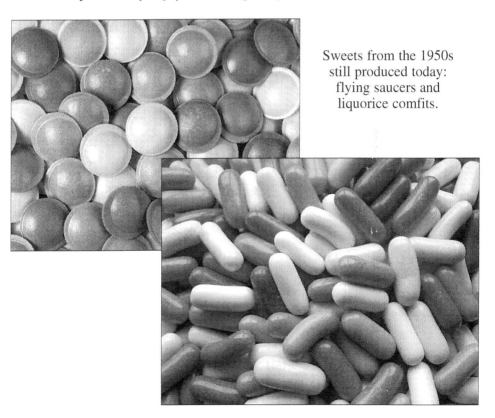

Sweets from the 1950s
still produced today:
flying saucers and
liquorice comfits.

The interior of a small shop of the 1950s. The cramped appearance resembles that of Florrie Bailey's shop, although her sweetshop was smaller.

This is obviously not a full list of 50s confectionery but it shows my extensive knowledge. This was of course my downfall as far as my teeth were concerned - I had to have quite a few fillings. These were done largely by a visiting mobile dentist that came around to the school in a great grey lorry cum haulage van which was especially kitted out as a dental surgery. It would park in the school playground. Each child would have their teeth checked over, then at a later time the van would return and administer the treatment. These were the early days of a national programme of dental treatment for schoolchildren done under the emerging National Health Service

Florrie Bailey, the shopkeeper, was a slight, good-humoured middle-aged lady who always wore a full-length floral cross-over pinafore over her woollen jumper and sensible skirt and booted feet. Her iron-grey bobbed hair was clipped back off her face. She was patient with her small school children customers who would crowd in after school, all holding out their open hands with pennies in them, hoping to be served first. She seemed to run her shop more as a community concern than a real business - most of her stock seemed to be sweets. Or was that just the focus of a 7 to 10 year old?

6. Visiting Billy Booth's Workshop.

My best friend at school was Margaret Booth. As you will remember from the Tizer episode of the first story, she was related to the elderly couple, Mr and Mrs Booth who lived on Park Lane, Knypersley. I think she was their great niece.

Unlike me, an only child, she was the youngest of four children and she lived locally, in fact her white, two storey cottage was at the end of the lane from the school, Hot Lane. It stood on the corner of Hot Lane and New Street and had quite a commanding view of central Biddulph Moor really. Her cottage looked out onto the police house and was near the post office, the Rose and Crown public house and Florrie Bailey's small corner shop - all essential amenities for Moorlanders. She was within fifty yards of the bus shelter and the roads that led down to Biddulph, Knypersley and Leek; transport arteries to other exotic places.

Margaret was a slight, blond, quick-witted, fun-loving child. The fact, that her father was the local garage owner and undertaker did not seem to weigh heavily on her shoulders. The gravity of her father's profession never really registered in my mind. If it had I might have been carried away with morbid and fanciful imaginings, but as it happened I was not. Often we would leave school at the end of the day and sprint the short distance to her cottage, laughing and giggling all the way. She would go into her house and I would walk on to the bus stop to await the service bus home.

One particular hot, sweaty, summer's day she asked me if I'd like to 'come in'. We had run all the way out of school, clutching our coats and schoolbags, and were quite hot and panting by the time we reached her house. Naturally I said 'Yes' as I wiped my sweaty forehead.

Now alongside the back entrance to her cottage lay a long, low brick building that you entered by 3 or 4 steps, this was just a short way away from the cottage's back door. And beyond that was her dad's small garage with a couple of petrol pumps. I didn't pay much attention to the brick building as we passed it but just went into her house, where her mother gave us a fizzy drink and an arrowroot biscuit. (Fizzy drinks in the 1950s seemed to young children and their parents to be the height of luxury and indulgence)

We greedily gulped down the drink, then panting, wiped the sweet liquid away from our lips with the back of our hands and wandered back outside, nibbling the biscuits around the edges. We trudged back to the odd few steps which led up to the outer building and sat down heavily on them. I say 'trudged' as there is a strange world weariness at times that only 8 year olds can achieve. After some more quiet moments of biscuit nibbling, Margaret broke the silent concentration, she had obviously been working out whether to ask the next question or not.

'Do you want to have a look in workshop?' she asked.

Not really knowing what a workshop was, I immediately said 'Yes.'

She stood up and ushered me to stand up off the step, opened the rough wooden door and peered in. 'Good,' she said 'nobody's about'.

So we proceeded to creep noiselessly and carefully inside. Inside, there was a dark gloominess despite the bright sunnyness of the day. The small windows must have been on the wrong side to receive the sun's radiance. It was quite a sizeable room I started to make out as my eyes grew accustomed to the low light, about the length of two garages put together, so a long rectangle of a room.

It felt chilly in there. Here and there I could make out lengths of different types of wood propped up against the walls. Shelves were fitted and contained small packets of materials. Brass handles were arranged on a low table. A workbench stood at one side, to the right of me. Margaret walked carefully in front of me in reverential silence. I followed gazing all about and bumped into her back, when she stopped suddenly without my noticing.

'Ouch,' she said.

'Sorry, Marg.'

'Well, this is it,' she said.

'Yes,' I agreed.

'You know what they do in here, don't you?'

I shook my head.

'It's the workshop for the ....yer know....' she nodded her head over to the left of the room. My eyes were becoming more adjusted to the shadowy shapes. Over in the direction of her nodding, I could make out quite a long wooden box perched on trestle supports. It looked like a bigger version of the Fyffe's banana box I'd seen bananas delivered in to my Mamma's shop. Just as I noticed it, Margaret finished her sentence. '....the coffins.' My young and finely tuned nervous system ground to a terrified halt! Surprisingly my feet continued to follow her as she went closer to the coffin. It was just like in a horror film where every fibre of your system is roaring for you to run away, in the opposite direction, yet still your body carries you relentlessly forward. I could only imagine the worst. We were going to view the body that lay within its well-crafted container. The dead body that lay within its coffin!

Margaret had by now got to within a few inches of the box and was gazing with a blissful look into it. My friend obviously had nerves of steel and was used to gazing on the bodies of those whose souls had already met God. I was not made of such strong stuff. 'I'll just, er, just stand here, if you don't mind,' I said.

'No, cum over here,' she persisted 'and have a look. It's beautiful.'

The word 'beautiful' drew my attention and seemed to overcome my thinly-disguised controlled terror. If I was going to see a dead person, let it be a beautiful one. And Margaret didn't seem to be scared stiff by what she was seeing. Then again I argued with myself she was obviously used to seeing this.... it.... bodies!

Bit by bit, I crept slowly forward, peering through my half-closed eyes, just to make sure I didn't trip over any work tools lying about. I stood next to Margaret's warm slim arm and at the side of the coffin.

'There,' she said. 'Just look what a beautiful job me Aunty Ethel makes of the linings. They're called shrouds, you know. That's what they put dead people in'

My eyes were tightly closed. 'Very nice,' I said.

'You've got yer eyes closed, so how do yer know? It's alright there's no body in it.... I wouldn't have come in if there was. My dad doesn't bring them here. They're in the chapel. Yer didn't think I was bringing yer in to see a dead body did yer? This is the workshop that's all - where they make the coffins.'

'Oh,' I sighed, a bit relieved, although I still wasn't convinced that I wanted to see inside a coffin either. I'd be thinking about it, the object, the box, all the rest of the day and probably the night!

'Me Aunty Ethel does all the 'material work for the deceased' - that's what me dad calls it anyway,' Margaret continued. 'All folds of white satin. It must make them look like angels. That's what I think.'

I edged closer to her. The little light in the room was shining through Margaret's short, blond, bubbly curls at the moment. She looked a bit like an angel herself. I noticed her peaceful expression so I bravely peered inside, and then gazed in at length. She was right. The box was lined with a beautiful, watery-smooth pure white material that lay in loose hilly folds especially at the box's narrow end. Nothing to be frightened of at all, but beautiful, as Marg had said. We looked at each other and smiled.

'Come on then,' she said, 'let's go play 'mirror' in the sun, before the bus goes.'

'Ok,' I replied and we quickly skipped out of the workshop and back into the bright sunlight which bathed us in its warmth. We walked further along the Booth's yard where there was more space to play and quickly fell into the game.

7. Relentless Rain and the Macclesfield Step

Two doors away from my grandma's shop, on the Biddulph Moor side, my mum and dad and I lived. It was number 67 Park Lane. My dad was a clerk in the offices at Whitfield Colliery and my mum helped my grandmother in the shop. Prior to my arrival she had worked in the Food Office in Biddulph, dealing with rationing coupons. Rationing didn't finish the minute WW2 did but went on for another 9 years. When she actually finished there I'm not sure.

The bungalow at 67 was roomy, detached, had a front and back garden and a garage and yard in which to park the grey Hillman car that my dad drove us all about in. That big bear of a car seemed huge to me as a young child. It certainly filled the yard when it was parked up and I remember with affection the running boards that you could stand on (not whilst it was going of course) that ran along the length of the doors at the bottom.

To get back to the bungalow layout. It had four main rooms that opened off from the black and white tiled corridor which ran from the front door. At the other end of the corridor was the very useful pantry where all groceries and foodstuffs were stored. (The advent of fridges and fitted kitchen units has done away with this room now in most modern homes. My Auntie Betty in Kingsfield Road, Biddulph still has her pantry in which she stores her goods despite having a fitted kitchen.) I think it is a much missed valuable room space. On the left as you stood at the front door was my mum and dad's bedroom. Opposite that door was the door to the front sitting room. Next to that on the right was the door into the kitchen and opposite the kitchen was my bedroom.

All of the furniture that we had, as I remember, was free standing - wardrobes and cupboards and kitchen cabinets for example. In my bedroom, I had a single bed, a free-standing wardrobe and set of drawers, maybe a chair and of course a grate for an open fire when the weather was very cold. In fact all the rooms except the bathroom had hearths for coal fires. (The bathroom had an electric bar heater high up on the wall.) My curtains were pink with large, repeated illustrations of Bambi on them. It was very cosy except of course when the wolves started to live under my bed. (My mum was never sure when I started to believe wolves lived under the bed, but there was a time when I could not get out of bed in the middle of the night because of the wolves!) I think I had a pink bedspread to match the other soft furnishings. Of course, the bedding was sheets,

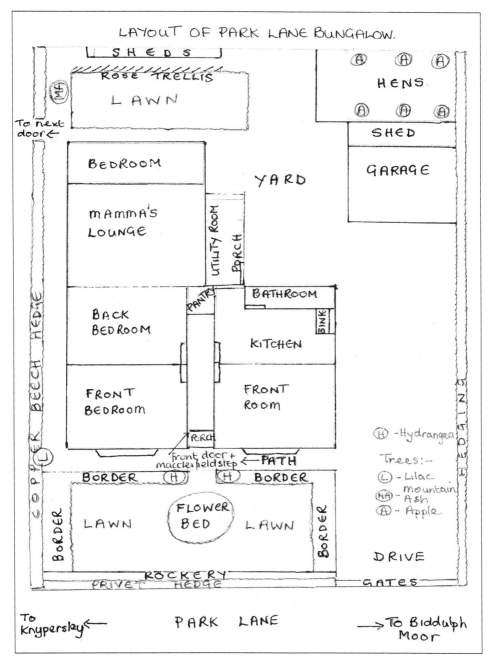

Layout of the Park Lane bungalow at number 67.

blankets, eiderdowns and tufty, candlewick bedspreads (they came in all colours) to throw over the top of the bedclothes. Duvets were undreamt of.

We had a green-tinged sink unit in the kitchen and off the kitchen was the bathroom. This had 2 (or more) external walls and in the winter, I can remember getting into the huge lead and white enamelled bath and sitting there with a freezing body above water and you guessed it, a warm body below water. (The wall heater seemed to have little effect in penetrating the Siberian chill of our bathroom.) Body temperatures in those days often encompassed the two extremes.

The bungalow had two bay windows at the front, one at the front bedroom and one in the living room. The garden at the front consisted of a square of lawn with borders around all the four edges. You would probably be able to park two cars on the space nowadays. At the left of the house were a white lilac tree and a mature laburnum tree which was spectacularly covered with its yellow hanging blossoms in the late spring. In the middle of the lawn was a round border of soil for annual planting. There was a low wall which retained the front garden and a small, slabbed, narrow access pathway which ran along the front of the house.

The bungalow had a small alcove porch with a low step up into the front passageway and it was here that the Macclesfield step was to be found. It was this sill that saved the bungalow from the cloudburst that rained down one summer Sunday in the 1950s and averted a calamitous flooding of the property. At least that's what I was led to believe by my mum, who, together with my dad and my cousin, Alan was in the house at the time of the deluge.

Production of Macclesfield Sills began at the Regent Foundry in Macclesfield in the late 19th century. The Foundry still stands, but production has now been transferred to the Regency Mill, itself a fine period Georgian Mill. The methods of production have kept pace with modern technology, but the Stormguard Sill retains the same proven design principals.

What happened on that relentlessly rainy Sunday afternoon, I am now about to relate.

It was a usual summer in that there was plenty of rain about. This Sunday's downpour was also accompanied by a resonant thunderstorm. These weather conditions frightened me and set my mother's nerves a-flutter. It didn't just rain either. Popular opinion afterwards concluded that it was a 'cloudburst'. It began innocently enough and unheeded of course. However as it persisted and got heavier, my mother noticed through the front room bay window that waves of water were starting to gush swiftly down our inclined pathway from the road. The guttering pipes couldn't contain the water draining from the roof and water began to overflow from them. Mini Niagaras poured down past the leaded windows. Our bungalow became like a ship riding stormy waves at sea.

I'm not sure why my dad decided to take a look outside the front door, (perhaps he thought a grid was getting blocked and so he would go and unblock it) but open the door he did. That's when the panic set in. As he opened the door, we saw that the water had lapped into the small storm porch and was beginning to climb its way up towards the next step that led inside the house!

'Oh God, Harry. What are we going to do?' I think were the next words uttered by my mother. 'If it comes in over the step, the whole house will be flooded. Oh my, what are we going to do? Do something.'

My father, not possessing the power of the Norse god Odin and being unable to turn tides at once, first just glanced helplessly at the lapping water. We all watched as it slowly began to creep higher and higher up towards the front door. The Macclesfield step would give the house another one and a half inches of safety but if it got over that, then the water was inside! The next thing to happen was that a bucket, jug and mop were located. As fast as the rain fell, the water could be scooped into the bucket and emptied down the sink. The mop was obviously an optimistic afterthought (it had gone past the mopping stage in the porch.)

My cousin Alan and I watched curiously at all these frantic operations, not understanding the full implication of a flooded house. Luckily, my Mamma was away for the day so was also not about to witness and get involved in the house saving operations. The bucket scooping operations were not making much of an impact on the depth of water. As fast as it was scooped up from the porch, it flooded in again from the path.

I am not sure how long this thankless flood defence activity went on for but just as my parents were beginning to accept defeat by the lapping water and the inevitable watery invasion... the rainfall began to get lighter! The water level had peaked in the porch with only a sheet of paper's depth to spare, before it climbed over the sill. We were saved from the second most serious flood since Noah's minor unpleasantness! Thank goodness we did not have to go rounding up various animals in pairs.

The afternoon wore on into tea-time and eventually although the rain had stopped, the water was still not draining away. What had happened to the grid system? My father went out to investigate. Nothing wrong with the small drains around the house, there was just too much water for them to cope, so what of the street grids? What were they doing? Had the rain just been too heavy for them to successfully divert the rainfall away? The mystery was soon solved, much to the annoyance of my dad. It turned out there had been some road works going on which had upset the camber of the road, causing the water to flood down our yard. The council had to be informed!

Slowly, but surely the flood water drained away. The Macclesfield step was praised often after the storm in such terms as, ' if it hadn't been for that step, we'd have been flooded out' and 'good job we had that Macclesfield step fitted or else....' By contrast the workmen carrying out the roadworks were severely taken to task for causing the near catastrophe in the first place.

My maternal great grandmother 'Grammy' in the middle of the picture and her two oldest daughters - Mamma on the left and my great Auntie Winnie on the right. Taken in the 1930s.

Below:
The three oldest sisters taken about the end of the 1950s. Great Auntie Cissie on the left (who ran the shop in Long Lane, Harriseahead); Great Auntie Winnie (centre) and Mamma on the right.
They are probably at a family wedding.

8. Grammy's Wednesday Visits

Every Wednesday evening my grandmother's mother, Grammy came to visit. Her full name was Elizabeth Ann Whalley and she came each Wednesday to have a white boiled ham sandwich supper (white sliced bread was the luxury then) a 'sninch' of cake (one of her own words, just a small slice) and a cup of tea with my grandmother and her sister to catch up on the family news. My mother and father would also look in and say 'hello' and I was always there during her visits. I can't remember which bungalow she used to visit exactly, but she had the choice.

My Mamma (grandmother) and great Aunt were her two oldest daughters. She had had four other children - three daughters and a son. Three other children had died as infants. In fact she had led a very hard life. Her husband, Christopher had died as a result of a mining accident in his late 30s leaving her with these six children to raise. To make money, she took in washing from a dentist in Tunstall and my Mamma and her sister, being the eldest siblings, went out to work to help to keep the family.

This was just after the end of the 1st World War and there were no social services then or widow's pension to cushion their lives. (Was it a land fit for heroes to return to?) My mother recalls that Gram seemed to be able to make good, hearty meals with very little ingredients that satisfied the family's appetites. Grammy had had practice in doing this since her own mother had died leaving her and a number of brothers at home. She had to cook and look after her father and brothers as a girl.

Despite her poverty and sadness, I remember her as a good-natured, twinkly lady with a fine, clear brain who was always ready to laugh. She had many wise sayings which she could summon up. Her definition of the monotony of housework for example was 'like threading beads without a knot on the end of the string.' She must have been resourceful and intelligent, not only just to survive the hand that fate dealt her but at the board school she attended, she was asked to stay on to teach and become qualified to do so - a role she had to decline to look after her brothers at home.

She was in her 70s when I began to know her and was under 5 feet tall, well rounded, always in a pinafore apron at home, (ie ready for action) wore a hairnet to keep her hair in order, and lived and still worked in another daughter's small shop until her last illness.

If ever a family bore out Napoleon's remark that 'England was a nation of small shopkeepers', my maternal family did. My grandmother ran several shops including grocery shops and a milliner's. My mother and father were to run two newsagent and grocery shops and an ironmonger's in the 1960s and 1970s. My great aunt ran a grocery shop on Long Lane, Harriseahead in the 1950s, 1960s and early 1970s. Another great aunt ran a shop.

During the 1950s and 1960s the only place to do the weekly shopping or rather daily shopping was at your small corner or local shop. Supermarkets in the 1960s were gradually starting but there was no proliferation of them until the late 1960s and early 1970s. As my mother said 'then you could see that the writing was on the wall for the end of the small shopkeeper.' So they got out of the shop-keeping business.

A particular memory I have of my Grammy is in Auntie Cissy's shop and her being asked to cut some bacon or boiled ham for a customer. They did have a mechanical bacon slicer but if a customer wanted the bacon thickly sliced, Grammy would hug the sizeable, string-bound bacon roll to her chest and then with a large carving knife proceed to cut the slices from the outside edge towards her own throat! Health and Safety laws, what were they? She never suffered any injury though and enjoyed her work in the shop. Small shops back then were part business, part social service, part gossip exchanges! In Harriseahead alone in the 1950s there were at least 5 small shops and a Co-op grocery store.

When Grammy visited Park Lane, we always had a fun evening. The entertainment I have to admit was supplied a lot by me. I remember my Shirley Bassey impressions went down very well. Ms Bassey in the 1950s tended to wear, (on such telly programmes as Sunday Night at The London Palladium) very fitted, glamorous, ankle-length, sparkling gowns. I attempted to imitate her attire by putting my two legs down one leg of my pyjama bottoms, (that got the fitted skirt effect) while twirling the other empty pyjama leg about (like a gown train) and belting out 'Kiss Me Honey Honey Kiss Me.'

Shirley Bassey, the singer from Tiger Bay, Cardiff in the 1960s.

I also performed a monologue 'Blow the Candle out' by a now unheard of comedian called Albert Modley. He was a Liverpudlian variety entertainer, well-known for his catch phrase 'Eeeeeehh! Isn't it grand when you're daft?!'

The 'Blow the Candle out' routine used to consist of him playing various family members, all of whom had some facial idiosyncracy which stopped them from blowing out the flame. For instance the father could only blow upwards, the mother could only blow to the left and so on. My mother says they used 'to be in stitches' listening to my version of his act. We were easily amused then.

The Liverpudlian comedian Albert Modley in the 1950s.

Early Bush TV set from the 1950s.

It is also interesting to note that although we had a small television set, probably a Bush model, back then in the 1950s, out of politeness for your guests' visit, it was switched off. You could then concentrate on your visitors and their news. The added factor that the TV screens were so small that it was difficult to see much action on them, unless you were perched only a few feet away, precluded many people watching successfully at the same time.

I was also very keen on drawing and drew members of my own family to sharpen my sketching skills. I remember a pencil drawing I did of my Grammy, I still have it in fact. It shows her left profile complete with hairnet, laughter lines around her eyes and a few nasal hairs. Her judgement on it was complimentary except for the nasal hairs, but she never asked me to alter the drawing.

Around 10.00 pm Grammy used to be collected by car by Aunty Cissie and her husband, Uncle Albert and they all went back home. They had been out for the evening and left Grammy visiting while they were out. Visiting time did not go on too late into the evening as both my grandmother and Aunties Winnie and

Cissy had to be up the next morning to open the shops and every one else was back into work.

Grammy was a dearly loved mother by all her children and extended family. She worked all her life, looked after her family loyally and died at the age of 83. She was never happier than when she was working and being useful. She was the first person whose death had an impact on my thoughts and life when I was fifteen. As they say today, she was an inspirational woman of goodness who set a positive example of living the best life that she could, despite her own personal setbacks and tragedies. She would have shrugged at those pompous words of praise and would have probably said 'oh, get off with you!'

My pencil drawing of Grammy, drawn during one of her Wednesday night visits to Park Lane, Knypersley. I must have been 10 or 11 when I did this, Grammy would have been in her late 70s.

Children gathered around a 1950s tv watching one of the most popular childrens' programmes of the time - Andy Pandy.

9. Mary Ellen Doorbar née Whalley

Mamma, in a studio-taken portrait,
as a young woman around 1920.

My mother's mother or 'Mamma', who ran this succession of small shops, was Mary Ellen Doorbar. She was born on the 29th December 1901 and died in November 1991 just one month short of her 90th birthday. She was 50 when I was born and as it turned out I was to be her only grandchild. She was quite a remarkable, strong, independently-minded woman. It was not that she chose to be this kind of person, but rather that the circumstances of her life had contrived to make her so.

Firstly, she was born the oldest child of nine that Grammy (Elizabeth Ann) and her husband, Christopher Charles Whalley, brought into the world. Two of those children died in infancy and one daughter, Alice, died in childhood. Of the remaining six there were five girls and one son. My Grammy was widowed in her thirties. Her husband Christopher, a miner, was injured in a pit accident and died as a result of his injuries. At the time my Mamma was 18 and together with her sister Winnie, they became the breadwinners for the family. My Grammy also took in washing from a dentist in Tunstall while my Mamma and Auntie Winnie became fustian cutters in one of the many local fustian (cotton) mills in the area. Of course Stoke-on-Trent was traditionally known for its 'pots, pits and service' industries. 'Service' referred to working in well-to-do households that needed cooks, maids, scullery staff and so on. What is forgotten about the area around here is that it was only about 20 miles from Manchester, or 'Cottonopolis' as it was known during its great industrial days, and around the Biddulph, Mow Cop and Congleton areas there were many small and medium-sized mills which especially worked with fustian. Dictionary definitions vary a little about fustian cloth but it was a type of rough fabric of stout twilled cotton or cotton and low-quality wool, with a short nap or pile.

From talking to my Mamma about those working days of hers I know that the fustian cloth was set out on frames in great long lengths and she and her fellow workers, armed with a long knife, walked around these long frames all their working day, cutting the nap on the cloth. Then it would be sent back to mills in Lancashire for further processing.

She said that during the course of the day, the girls would walk miles in their clogs around these long frames cutting the cloth pile. Then they would have to walk or bike back home after their long working day of 10 or 11 hours.

My grandmother married on Boxing Day 1927. There were no photographs taken at the time. She delayed her marriage to James Doorbar until she was nearly 26 which for that day and age was quite a mature age. She wanted to make sure that all her sisters and her brother reached maturity and were able to stand 'on their own two feet' before she set up her own home. The role of 'big sister' however was a role which she would play throughout the rest of her life. She felt a sense of responsibility for her own first, nuclear family and helped them all out financially, emotionally and practically many times.

During the course of her marriage to Jim, my Mamma went on to own a small grocery shop in Long Lane, Harriseahead while Jim worked down the pit. During World War II, my grandfather also served as an ARP warden but during the course of the conflict, he contracted tuberculosis and died in 1943 in a local sanatorium over towards Leek. My mother was just 14, and both her and my Mamma, were distraught to breaking point. My Mamma herself thought that she experienced an emotional collapse. She was only 42 and facing the prospect of earning her living as a single parent raising a teenager.

There was no 'emotional counselling' in those days and the war was still dragging on with many other casualties, so there was no choice but to 'go on.'

She often spoke of his death and believed that his health was affected by his imprisonment in Belgium during the First World War. He had 'joined up' under age and was only a teenager at the time. At a crucial time in his physical development when he should have been having 'good food' he was deprived of this and was virtually starved as a prisoner of war. This she believed weakened his constitution and led to his early death at the age of 44.

My Mamma was not a woman who let her imagination run away with her but there is a strange incident that both her and my mother experienced independently, a short time after grand-dad Jim's death. They had taken themselves to the cinema in Biddulph to lighten their mood; to forget their personal grief and the country's troubles for an hour or two. What they experienced next they kept to themselves for some time because they both thought that it was a trick of their imagination and just wishful thinking. However, just before the end of the film a man got up in front of them in the darkness and waved and smiled at them while they were still seated. The man was granddad Jim, their husband and father, leaving the picture-house and taking his leave of them for the last time (it seemed.) At the time neither of them said anything to the other. Both were stunned but thought it was just a trick of the light, a man who looked like James Doorbar. Yet by his manner and appearance he was Jim and seemed to be telling them that he was alright and not to worry. Some time elapsed before they confessed seeing him but both were convinced this was a loving, spiritual experience from a recently deceased man who did not want to leave his family so soon.

Life moved on and in 1944 Mamma had bought a home, and a milliners and ladies' drapers shop in Biddulph High Street, next to Arthur Barker's, the butchers. My mother and father had met and were married in December 1949. By 1950 my Mamma had moved to the grocery shop in Park Lane. She was joined by my mother and father and her sister, my great Auntie Winnie, who also worked in the shop. Then of course I was born in 1951 and my experience of small shop-keeping and the world began.

When I remember Mamma, I remember a woman who was a pocket dynamo. She was about 5 feet tall (at her tallest and in her prime she would tell mc.) She had greying hair, a well-proportioned handsome face, a well-rounded figure, she was talkative, could be argumentative and bossy, and never stopped working in some capacity or other. She worked all her life and at one stage as well as shop-keeping she owned houses which relatives lived in. Had she been born fifty years later, and had the advantage of a higher education, she might have been a successful professional woman. As it was she pulled herself out of considerably poverty to own her own homes and businesses and remain an independently-minded woman.

She missed her husband Jim all the rest of her life and talked about him often. She missed his easy-going nature and sense of fun which could lighten moods and I imagine he served as a good counterpoint to her serious character. My admiration knows no bounds for what she achieved in her life despite adversity along the way.

As a child, I remember her as a caring grandmother who made me 'beef tea' to 'build up my strength' when I was not well. She fed me my favourite dessert of red jelly and evaporated milk when, as a fussy small child, I would arrive back from school and would eat little else that was offered to me. (She could never give me green jelly, I just would not touch it.) She provided me with numerous bottles of Lucozade to tempt my appetite; made vast vats of the local dish of lobby to keep us all nourished in the winter and clothed me in many of her hand-knitted cardigans, hats and scarves. These kept me warm throughout the bitter winters that swept over a Moorland countryside that could resemble Siberia at times.

What my mamma witnessed during the first 60 years of the 20th century.

I think it is fascinating to record the pace and the abundance of change in political, social and scientific terms that my grandmother lived through during the first 60 years in the twentieth century. She went from biking or riding up and down in a pony and trap as a girl, to 'charabang' day trips, then car excursions and swift train travel. Although she never experienced aeroplane travel herself, she watched as the nation experienced their first package holidays abroad. She watched men develop transatlantic air flight and then fly to the moon. Life must have become to her the 'stuff of dreams.'

She witnessed two world wars, a general strike and the birth of a National Health Service. She remembered seeing Halley's Comet appear in the skies in April 1910 when she was an 8 year old and sitting on the step of her home in Biddulph. Some uncle gave her the bottom from a bottle to look at the phenomenon through so that she would not hurt her eyes. She witnessed its return in 1986, just like the American writer Mark Twain who witnessed it twice in his lifetime also. (He died a day after the comet's appearance in 1910 having been born two weeks after its appearance in 1835.) Twain died as my mamma sat watching it on her house step in Biddulph.

My mamma watched as the world changed from a straight-laced Victorian, society of the early 1900s, to a liberal, swinging culture of the 1960s. She watched as chapel-going on Sundays gave way to Sunday afternoon car excursions. She witnessed the rise of the 'teenager' as a social entity and saw the spirit of rebelliousness grow in the country with its questioning of traditional values. To me, she took all of these changes in her stride and while she did not like some developments, never-the-less took them into account, adapted and survived.

A brief resume now follows of some of the key events from 1901 to 1963, the course of my mamma's life, and some of the years covered by this book.

Key events of my Mamma's life

1901 January   Queen Victoria dies and Edward V11 becomes King.
       March   The first diesel motor on public display.
       May   The population of Britain 41.5 million.
       December New era of global communications when Guglielmo Marconi, the Italian pioneer of wireless, transmits a message across the Atlantic.

Mamma - Mary Ellen Whalley born.

1903 October   Manchester: the militant campaign for women's suffrage began led by Mrs Emmeline Pankhurst. Their motto 'Deeds not Words.'

1904 March   First electric main-line train in the British Isles from Liverpool to Southport.
       May   The Honourable Charles Rolls signs agreement to make cars with Henry Royce.

1905 March   By public demand Sir Arthur Conan Doyle's new book describes Sherlock Holmes' return from death.
       October   Aspirin goes on sale for the first time.

1906 March   Principle of old age pensions approved by Parliament British Empire occupies a fifth of the world's land surface.

1909   Old age pensions for people over 70.
February   Colour films screened in Britain for first time.
April   Cheshire: first closed top double decker buses in Britain.
July   Louis Bleriot first man to fly across the Channel.

1910   May   Edward VII dies, George V succeeds him
August   Florence Nightingale dies

Mamma witnesses Halley's comet.

1912   April   The 'unsinkable' transatlantic liner 'Titanic' sinks.

1914   August   War declared on Germany.
September Government calls for a further 500,000 volunteers to serve
their country.
October   Trenches dug across Europe in a 'new type of warfare.'

1915   December   Gallipoli, Allied forces retreat from disaster.
War encircles the globe.
Women play bigger part in the war effort as they take over
men's roles. 1 million more women working full-time.

1916   October   On Western Front British casualties estimated at 350,000.
November   Slaughter at the Battle of the Somme.

1918   February   Women over 30 and men over 21 gain right to vote.
March   Minimum school leaving age raised to 14.
November   Peace declared. 750,000 men from Britain and 200,000
from the Empire killed in the Great War. 1.5 million
seriously injured.

1919   January   Scientists show how to split the atom.
March   Influenza epidemic has killed 150,000 people.
December   Nancy Astor first woman M.P.

*Mamma's father dies as a result of a mining accident. She
is working as a fustian cutter.*

1921   March   First birth control clinic opened in London as a result of Dr
Marie Stopes' work.

1921 August   British women outnumber men by 2 million.

1922 November Daily wireless broadcasts planned by the B.B.C.

1923 April   Duke of York marries Lady Elizabeth Bowes-Lyon.

1924 January   Labour Party comes to power for first time. Ramsey
MacDonald Prime Minister.
         April   Britain has first national airline, Imperial Airways.

1926 January   First ever widows' pensions paid out at post offices.
John Logie Baird demonstrates 'television', sending
moving pictures by radio.
         May   TUC calls general strike.

On Boxing Day mamma married James Doorbar.

1927   'Talking pictures' at the cinema. Going to the cinema a very
popular leisure-time activity.

1929 July   *My mother is born.*

1930 May   Amy Johnson first woman to fly across the world.
         December A draft Highway Code issued.

1934 March   New drivers have to pass a driving test.

1936 January   George V dies, Edward VIII becomes king.
         December Edward VIII abdicates to marry the American divorcee Mrs
Simpson. Duke of York, Bertie, becomes George VI.
         August   First TV broadcast from Alley Pally (Alexander Palace) by
BBC.

1939 September Britain at war with Germany. Children are evacuated from
all major cities to the countryside and abroad.

1940 January   2 million men called up to serve the country.
Food rationing begins with butter, sugar and bacon.
         May   All-party coalition rules the country
         July   Home Guard. Veteran soldiers enrolled to defend Britain's shores.

My Grandad Jim Doorbar enrolled as Air Raid Warden
(ARP) on duty during enemy bombing raids

1940 September RAF chase the German Luftwaffe back across the Channel during the 'war in the skies'- the Battle of Britain.

1941 December Female conscription announced to combat labour shortage (unmarried women in their 20s.) They were to join the police and fire brigades and non-combat roles like Land Army producing food.
Blitz on UK cities
Britain declares war on Japan after Pearl Harbour.

1942 March   Coal, gas and electricity rationed.
December 'Welfare State' proposed to care for people 'from the cradle to the grave' by Sir William Beveridge.

1943 May   German and Italian forces North Africa surrender to Allies

Grandad Jim Doorbar dies from tuberculosis.

1944 January Bevin Boys start training down the mines.
May   Allied invasion of Europe imminent.
June   Normandy 'D-Day' landings.

Mamma buys a milliner's and ladies'
clothes shop in Biddulph

1945 May   VE Day (Victory in Europe.)
August   VJ Day (Victory over Japan.) The War ends
December Britain signs agreement for International Monetary Fund and World Bank.

1946 March   Bank of England nationalised.
Bananas available at Covent Garden market for first time since war began.
Plans for free school milk and dinners.
May   Student grants introduced.
November House of Lords told 'tidal wave' of divorce sweeping country.
December Plans announced to nationalise railways, iron and steel.

1947 January   Coal nationalised.
Freezing weather and a fuel crisis bring industry to near standstill.
August   First atomic reactor at Harwell.
September School leaving age raised to 15.
November Princess Elizabeth marries Lieutenant Philip Mountbatten.

1948 January   Mahatma Gandhi assassinated.
April   Electricity nationalised. New GCE examination for England and Wales.
May   The birth rate booms
July   National Health Service begins, including dental services.
August   First Olympic games since 1936 staged in London.
November Prince Charles born.

1949 March   Chocolate, sweet and clothes rationing ended.
May   Gas industry nationalised.
September   The Pound devalued.

December - my mother and father married.

1950 February   Labour Party clings to power in General Election.
March   Survey shows only 46% of homes have a bathroom.
May   Petrol rationing ends
July   First self-service store opened by J. Sainsbury.

Mamma buys the grocery shop on Park Lane, Knypersley.

1951 May   Old age pensions paid to men over 65 and women over 60.
The Festival of Britain opened to showcase Britain.
October   Churchill becomes Prime Minister again at 77.
December Television spreads to northwest of England.

*May - I was born, Mamma's granddaughter and
Grammy's oldest great grandchild.*

1952 February   George VI dies, Princess Elizabeth becomes Elizabeth II.
Britain tests Atom Bomb
December First British film in technicolour, Genevieve.
Queen Mary dies.

1953 March   Francis Crick and American James Watson identify DNA.
          April   Queen Elizabeth II crowned. Mount Everest conquered by
          June   Edmund Hillary and Sherpa Tensing led by Sir John Hunt.
          November Birth of independent TV company, ITV

1954 May   Roger Bannister ran first sub 4 minute mile.
          July   Rationing ends
          December Building of houses breaks all records.

1955 January   Millions to be spent on electrifying and building new
                    railways.
          July   Clean Air Act.
                    Teddy Boys a youth phenomenon.
          September ITV begins - with adverts between programmes.

1956 April   Premium Bonds introduced to encourage saving.
          September African colonies to have freedom from the British Empire.
          November Suez crisis. Confrontation between Egypt and Britain,
                    France/Israel, World opinion forces Britain, France and
                    Israel to withdraw.

1957 March   Britain says 'No' to Common Market in Europe.
          April   National Service ends.
          July   New IRA campaign of violence in Ireland begins.
          November Jodrell Bank, space telescope, opens in Cheshire.
          December Rock and roll music craze.

1958 February 'Busby Babes', Man Utd, die in Munich plane crash.
          April   First CND march against nuclear weapons Aldermaston.
          June   Yellow lines introduced onto roads to stop parking.
          July   Vaccination against polio introduced.
          September Race riots in two English cities.
                    BOAC first transatlantic flight.
          December LPs (long playing records), STD telephone system and
                    Hovercraft invented.

1959 January   'Teenagers,' a new phenomenon.
          May   'Cod War' over fishing between Britain and Iceland.
          August   'Mini' car launched.
                    Supersonic Concorde to be developed with France.

1960   February   Princess Margaret married Antony Armstrong-Jones.
         May   Cyprus became independent. RSC (the Royal Shakespeare
         August   Company) formed at Stratford under Peter Hall.

1961   January   Contraceptive pill available in Britain
                   South Africa leaves the Commonwealth.
         July   Yuri Gagarin, Russian cosmonaut, visits Britain.
         October   Malta gains independence.

1962   February   Anti-nuclear protestors jailed.
         April   Push-button Panda crossings introduced.
         May   Coventry Cathedral opened. The original destroyed during
                   Second World War.
         August   Sir Lawrence Olivier first director of the National Theatre.
         October   First James Bond film.

My mamma had given up shop-keeping in Park Lane.

1963   February   Harold Wilson labour prime minister commits to scientific
                   revolution to advance Britain's role in the world -'the
                   white heat of technology.'
         March   Branch lines axed by Dr Beeching.
         June   'Profumo scandal' - involving sexual indiscretions, MPs,
                   high society and national security.
         August   The Great Train Robbery £2.6 million stolen (equivalent
                   to £40 million today)

         November   Beatlemania sweeps
                   the country.

A pencil drawing I did of the
Beatles in 1966

The Wedding of Auntie Alice and Uncle George in the early 1950s.
Left to right: Mrs Allmark (Uncle George's mother), Uncle George's brother, Uncle George,
Auntie Alice, Uncle Bill, cousin Laura, my Dad, Grandma Berrisford. I was only 3 or 4 and
wearing a lovely white dress with rosebuds on but refused to have my picture taken.

Myself and Hazel as bridesmaids at Valerie and Jim's Wedding in March 1960.

10. Being a Bridesmaid

Probably one of the most exciting things to happen to a little girl in the 1950s was to be a bridesmaid. Although I was an only child and my mother was an only child, I did get the chance to be a bridesmaid a number of times as a girl because of the number of cousins in my mother's extended family, of all ages.

Of course couples got married in those days, they did not 'live together.' They had a wedding to celebrate their union and that was most often conducted in church or chapel. Young women wore the traditional white wedding dress and liked to have not just one or two bridesmaids but as many as they could. Up to the age of 19, I was a bridesmaid on four occasions. (I was a bridesmaid after that age on 3 more occasions, so I have done my fair share of bridal duties.) I think the one occasion I remember most vividly was being a bridesmaid to my mother's younger cousin, Valerie.

Valerie married Jim in Tunstall Roman Catholic Church in the middle of March and it was a very lovely white wedding. I was 9 at the time and my dress was especially bought for the day. It was beautiful and resembled a miniature crinoline. It was a white, sleeveless, floor-length nylon dress with a full silk lining. This lining from the waist down was covered and draped with folds of fine, stiffened netting and then over the top of that (from the waist) was a ruched shorter panel of material (the crinoline bit.) At the base of each ruched swag was a couple of blue daisy flowers, daisy-sized. At the top of the fitted bodice, on the shoulders were these same daisy flowers and a small white bow. It had two long, lovely, wide sash ribbons that were integral to the bodice front. They tied into a lovely bow at the back of the dress. I wore a small coronet of the same blue daisies around my head, with a blue silk

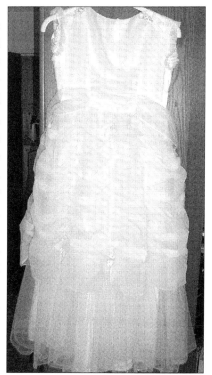
The bridesmaid's dress which I wore at Valerie's Wedding.

Valerie and Jim's Wedding at Tunstall R.C. Church.
Left to right: Evelyn, Hazel, the best man, Mrs Bell (Jim's mother), Mr Bell (his father), Jim, Valerie, Auntie Cissie (Valerie's mother), Uncle Albert (her father), me and another bridesmaid friend.

ribbon hanging down at the back. I had white silk pumps. There were the two of us dressed in that fashion- myself and Hazel. We carried two fresh, spring flower posies tied with a white ribbon. There were two older bridesmaids dressed alike but differently from us. I felt like a little princess for the day and an impressive, fairy tale entourage we made, I would suggest.

Valerie's dress too was a crinoline style. Naturally, it was a long, white full gown with tiered lace panels at the front. Her lacy bodice and sleeves were very fitted. She had a lovely tiara of white flowers with a net veil attached, which I can only remember hanging down her back. (I am not sure if she came into the church service with this veil over her face - or does that just happen in films really?) Her spray of roses and spring flowers were fresh, be-ribboned and triangular. The size of the bouquet had become more modest in the 1950s and 1960s. Dress necklines were modest. We all wore gloves. The older bridesmaids' gloves were elbow length, while my gloves and Hazel's were wrist length.

Jim, the bridegroom and his best man, his father and father-in-law, all wore smart dark lounge suits with a white carnation and fern buttonhole. The mothers of the bride and groom were dressed in smart suits, corsages and were hatted. The official photographer was John Martin of Hanley and Leek. Everyone on each of his successively-larger photographs amazingly was facing the right way and smiling.

Of course, I don't remember much of the day itself except it went very well. I do remember that it was such a cold, if dry March day, that when I was not having my picture taken by the official photographer, I had a shawl around me. In one of the larger group photographs, my Grammy was standing behind me with her arms around my shoulders in an attempt to keep me warm.

The next year, but this time in the summer, I was to be a bridesmaid for another of my mother's cousins, Evelyn. The interesting part of the occasion this time was that my dress was especially made for me (following the pattern of my second cousin, Doreen's existing bridesmaid's dress) and for my measurements and subsequent fittings I had to go to a dressmaker's house in Brown Lees. Unfortunately, I do not know the lady's name. This white dress again had a full, floor length skirt and fitted bodice. The material had an embossed little flower pattern running throughout it and my neckline this time was more adventurous. It had a wide rectangular panel which framed my face. My only niggle about this was that while my cousin Doreen's collar lay flat against her shoulders, mine would not.

This time there were six bridesmaids - two older ones in peach satin; myself and Doreen who were 10 and two smaller bridesmaids still who were 4-5 years of age. This was quite a retinue for Evelyn, another lovely bride who married Arnold in the summer of 1961. The service was held at Newchapel Church as Evelyn was a Harriseahead girl.

Evelyn's Wedding Day.
Another cousin of my mother's, here with her retinue of bridesmaids. I am on the left and Evelyn's younger sister Doreen (a great playmate in my childhood) is on the extreme right.

"Standard" FIREWORKS

HUDDERSFIELD, ENGLAND.

TO GET THE BEST RESULTS ALWAYS FOLLOW THE DIRECTIONS MARKED ON THE FIREWORKS

HERE ARE A FEW GOOD TIPS:—

Jumping Crackers — perform their best antics on hard ground or paving.

Pin Wheels — Use a strong pin fixed firmly to a post. Fix the pin to slope very slightly downwards from the post. This keeps the wheel near the head of the pin and prevents it binding against the post.

Pom-Pom Cannons — The warning spurt of sparks is for 5 seconds before the bang.

Flyers or Flying Imps — Stand clear when you have lit the touchpaper as they fly in any direction.

Roman Candles & Long Fountains — Fix them firmly in an upright position by pushing them into soft earth.

Volcanos, Mount Vesuvius and Short Fountains — Stand them on a level surface before lighting.

Air Bombs and Star Shells — Fix them firmly in an upright position, clear of buildings and overhead obstructions.

Wear an old glove for those marked "to be held in the hand."

Never get over the top of a firework to light it (or after you have lit it). Light it at arms length.

"Standard Fireworks" Ltd., Huddersfield.

An operational guide from Standard fireworks when lighting fireworks.

11. Bonfire Night at Auntie Al's

When I was a child in the 1950s, I don't remember there being any organised, communal bonfire parties in the towns or villages to go to. Parents would buy boxes of Standard fireworks for their children and set them off themselves in their backyards with maybe a small bonfire burning as well. Other relatives with children would be invited to share the evening and entertainment. Baking potatoes would be wrapped in silver foil and put into the bonfire flames for at least an hour to cook through; sausages would be grilled inside the house and put into buns to make hotdogs. Toffee apples were eaten. The food would be simple, warming and filling which was very fitting for the night which really symbolised the beginning of the dark, cold winter season ahead.

My family kept small shops so setting a box of fireworks aside for our use was easy enough. Fireworks were often sold loose as well. I know that we kept the loose ones in a glass cabinet so people could see and choose what they wanted to buy but they were safely enclosed so were not a temptation for small children to steal. There was a lot of concern about the dangers from fireworks and the burns they could cause back then.

I had several favourites: roaring rockets that were launched into the night sky from milk bottles; pretty Catherine wheels that had to be nailed onto line posts to spin at their best; brown innocent-looking S-shaped jumping jacks that once set alight seemed to follow me squealing all around the dark yard. (I don't think you can buy these now, they must be regarded as too dangerous.) You had to have a sparkler always lit as well; in fact two were the best, one for each hand. Then, you could write and spell out your name in fire in the air with the glowing, smouldering sticks. I loved chrysanthemum fountains which erupted gently in a shower of white, yellow and orange sparks which then cascaded to the ground. Traffic Lights were spectacular as they fired their red, then orange and finally green sparkling displays high into the air at unexpected moments.

To be on the safe side you put the used fireworks into a bucket of sand or water. An exciting if nervous moment in the whole evening might arrive when my dad lit the blue touch paper of a firework and after a number of seconds instead of bursting and burning in its multi-coloured way; the flame sputtered and died out. Then the decision had to be taken whether it was safe to go back and relight it. Had it really gone out or was it still smouldering secretly away ready to catch out my unsuspecting dad? We never had any accidents but never-the-less my mother would still anxiously say 'Be careful Harry, you don't know if it really has gone out.' And most fireworks did work, there were very few disappointments.

There was one Bonfire Night however which did not go according to plan. This particular Guy Fawkes' Night we were invited to spend it at my Auntie Alice's and Uncle George's. Auntie Alice was my dad's older and only sister and she and Uncle George lived in a bungalow higher up Park Lane, along Mill Hayes Road. They had plenty of space behind their house for a bonfire and a firework display. My dad had brought a box of 10 shilling fireworks from the shop with a few extra rockets for excitement and these were put immediately we arrived for safety into a tin box with a lid in the back porch at the back of Aunt Al's bungalow.

Meanwhile my dad and Uncle George were setting up the dark back garden for the ensuing display; milk bottles were being found as rocket launchers, posts and nails prepared for Catherine wheels. Inside the rest of us were either watching the preparations through the kitchen window (me) or getting a spot of hot food ready (my mum and Auntie Alice.) I think we watched a few chrysanthemum and silver fountains, and then it was time for a more spectacular firework- a rocket! I can't remember who placed the rocket in the bottle launcher but it seemed to be unstable from the beginning of the operation. As Cape Canaveral might have said 'Huston we have a problem'.

The blue touch paper was lit; the rogue rocket sputtered, flew about a foot from the ground and immediately took refuge in the back porch and found a resting place in the tin box with all the dry fireworks yet to be lit! Needless to say the lid had been left off the tin box thinking the fireworks were perfectly safe there! And what a display we had for about a minute and a half - multicoloured lights, sparks, bangs, pops and whizzings. My dad and Uncle George must have had a good view as they retreated out into the garden away from the porch. Inside the back kitchen of course we had to close off the door into the porch to keep the rockets and jumping jacks from invading the house!

It could have turned into a nasty incident but it did not. The only damage at the end of 'the impromptu display' was a smoked out and wall-blackened porch luckily. However I think my crying must have rivalled the firework noise as I complained noisily that 'they were all gone up in smoke and I didn't see them properly. Wah.' My father had to rush out to a nearby late opening shop and try and get another box-which he managed to do. What a hero. The evening then continued as planned with no more setbacks.

12. Uncle George's Bubble Car

My Uncle George always drove interesting vehicles back in the 1950s and 1960s. They always seemed quirkier choices than anyone else we knew. For instance I remember him driving not only a black motorbike but one that had a two-seater sidecar attached for Aunt Alice to sit in. (She did ride pillion but not all the time.) Later on he had a succession of three-wheeler Reliant Robins. His choices stemmed from the fact that he only ever held a motorcycle driving licence, so this limited his transport selection. However to my cousin Alan and I as children, when we were taken out by Auntie Alice and Uncle George, it was always going to be an interesting journey and day.

I remember for instance one trip when Alan and I were in the sidecar, we were driving along the road from Biddulph Moor to Rudyard and were going along the narrow bilberry-lined lanes on that slow, bendy descent to Rudyard Lake. Well, one particular bend Uncle George didn't quite make and we ended up slowly running into one of the grassy slopes at the roadside. He wasn't doing a great speed and we just came to a sedate thump into the verge-side. Of course Auntie Alice on the pillion was quite put out but for Alan and I it was all part of the day's entertainment. We laughed, none the worse for wear, got out and picked some bilberries and then Uncle George drove on.

Auntie Alice also related one event-packed journey that they had made back from Cornwall with horror. (In the 1960s Cornwall was a long journey to make - there was not the motorway network that exists today. Often when my mum and dad and I made the trip we would break the journey by staying in a B and B somewhere after Bristol on our way to Newquay. The length of the journey then only serves to emphasize Auntie Alice's discomfort.)

The first thing to go dramatically wrong was that the window screen shattered in their Reliant Robin - not a mechanical fault so they could travel on northwards. (There was no window replacement callout service in those days.) Things took a turn for the worse when it began to rain. The rain wasn't a light shower, it began to bucket down and despite having raincoats they got wet. To cap the experience as they were nearing home and passing through a small village a carnival procession was in progress. They couldn't overtake the procession so had to join the back of it as though they were part of it. 'I've never been so ashamed,' my Auntie Alice commented finally.

The other memorable thing about my Uncle George's cars was that something always seemed to be going wrong with them and my Uncle Bill (Auntie Alice's brother) was often called out as a travelling mechanic to help to try and solve the problem.

However, as a child, the car I most associated him and Aunt Al with was his three wheeled, grey bubble car. I do not know the make or model, being a child at the time. My cousin Alan (who was and still is mad about cars,) will probably know the make and model. Uncle George's car had the one large front door which you opened to get into

The 1960s BMW bubble car.

the vehicle. It was very much like the illustration. It was a bit like opening a door hatch into a cellar. It opened upwards and outwards and then you dived into the seats as opposed to falling down the cellar.

Where Uncle George's differed was that his whole roof was one entire bubble of domed, plastic window. It was an amazing car. It had two seats: - the driver's at the front and at the back a seat big enough for me and my cousin Alan to sit in (when we were both under 10.) My Uncle George was also a well-made chap so when he got in the car sagged considerably. On a warm summer's day it could get pretty hot under the plastic dome but there were little side windows to open, so there was ventilation. The plastic dome I also remember had a yellowy tinge to it so it was like wearing tinted spectacles when you viewed the scenery from the car. However not only did you get a good view of passing traffic but you could view the sky, birdlife and passing aeroplanes with ease as well. Alan and I were often transported from Auntie Alice's on Mill Hayes Road, Knypersley to our Grandma Berrisford's on John Street in Biddulph.

My Grandma Berrisford was a widow and had three children:- my Auntie Alice (the oldest), my Uncle Bill and then my dad, Harry, who was the youngest. Four years separated each child which used to make it easy for me to calculate everybody's ages from the starting point of my dad's age. She lived on her own in John Street in the middle of Biddulph and had looked after the home and her

My dad struggling to hold myself
and cousin Alan (on the right)
outside Grandma Berrisford's
back door on John Street,
Biddulph in 1953.

An extended family holiday
probably in Blackpool about
1949/50.
Left to right: Auntie Winnie,
Grandma Berrisford, Mamma and
Mum with Stafford at the front.

children all her married life.
John Street had been the home
she had lived in since her
marriage and to me it seemed
quite a big, dark, forbidding
house and it had an upstairs
which to me was a novelty as I
lived in a bungalow.

I should add that the house
may have been forbidding but my
Grandma certainly was not. She
was a quiet, gentle woman of a
very placid nature. When I
visited, occasionally I would
accompany her upstairs to collect
some small thing. The stairwell
was very dark and wood-lined
and smelt strongly of paraffin
because my Grandma would take
a small oil lamp upstairs with her
when she went to bed. I'm not
sure why she just didn't turn the
electric lights on or have a small
lamp on through the night but
anyway she liked to have the
little paraffin lamp burning to
give her some light to see by

Studio portrait of Grandad and Grandma Berrisford
with their two sons - my Uncle Bill and my dad (seated)
c. 1938/39.

during the night. This was the 1950s and 1960s I am talking about so
economising might well have been on her mind. Once we got upstairs there were
three bedrooms and she slept in the back one. The corridor down to this back
bedroom was narrow and dark and to me spooky, but she seemed at home with it.

My Auntie Alice would be at her mother's helping out and Alan and I would
go along to visit. Once there we would often be offered a slice of my Grandma's
home-made apple pie. This would often come served hot from the oven in the
fire range and was delicious. The range oven that my grandma had was an oven
which was heated by the coal fire and it was integral to the hearth and fire. No

one else I knew when I was a little girl had this kind of oven. My Grandfather Berrisford had been a collier and as his widow my Grandma was entitled to free coal from the NCB (National Coal Board.) This powered the range and always meant that there was a good fire blazing in her hearth. On the hearth in front of the fire my Grandma's homemade rag rugs would take pride of place. These would be made from an old sack or piece of sacking and onto it as a base, pieces of cut rags, cut to the same length would be threaded and knotted. My Grandma seemed to make up her own attractive patterns and designs.

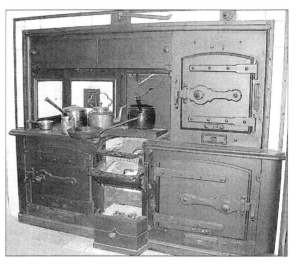

A fire range of the 1940s. My Grandma Berrisford's was half this size with the open fire and the integral oven attached to the left of it.

Washing equipment in the early 1950s: Grandma had the washing tub, wash board and dolly peg (for agitating the clothes), but not the hand mangle; she wrang the water out of the clothes by hand in the kitchen sink. The clothes would then hang out in the back yard to dry - or in the kitchen if it was wet.

Suspended from the ceiling in the living room was her wooden clothes airer, which often would have neatly ironed and folded clothing and linen on it. She would wash her clothes in a big tub, set on the kitchen floor and have a dolly peg to agitate them and get them clean. She would rinse them and then hand ring everything in the sink before hanging them out to dry, weather permitting. What she did when there was no good drying weather, I'm not sure.

It was also a treat when I was at my Grandma's to be given the long toasting fork with a piece of bread spiked on to the end and to sit making my own toast in front of her open fire. I was entrusted to do this job from quite an early age, although constantly warned not to get too close to the fire 'because we don't want any accidents.' Once the bread was browned on both sides I could then lavish it in butter and sit eating it in front of her small screen telly.

If it was a Saturday and around 5 o'clock we would not watch the telly but we would sit with the radio on quite loudly while my Grandma checked her Vernon's football coupon. I think the announcers on Radio 2 still declare the league results in the same style as the announcer used in the 1950s. He would raise the tone of his voice to indicate which team had won the match ie Stoke- 2 (announcer's voice rose in tone) Wolverhampton -nil (announcer's voice dipped in tone.) I always liked the sound of the announcements of the Scottish football league especially when they got to those results which might go: 'Forfar- 4, Queen of the South-5' and 'Hamilton Academicals' always struck me as a wonderful name for a football team. I don't know if my Grandma ever won anything much 'on the pools' but certainly she entered her coupon on which she forecast the results for years. I remember her sitting in deep concentration and

A Vernon's Football Pool's entry form from the 1950s.

licking the end of her pencil as she checked them off.

The other great rival to Vernons was Littlewoods pools. Both of them operated out of Liverpool. They are still running today but have been overtaken in popularity by the National Lottery as a means to a fortune. There can be some skill involved with the 'pools' as knowledge of football is involved to try and predict the outcome of the teams' Saturday fixtures.

My grandma also had a front room which you stepped into immediately when coming in through the front door. This was 'kept for best' and used just for high days, holidays and if any company arrived. It had a bay window which looked out onto John Street and in it there was a large brown leather-type sofa with two matching armchairs. There was a small table at the side of the door and a cold store next to the door into the scullery (main living room). Grandma's cold store was her fridge box in which she stored a few perishable items like butter and cheese and milk. On top of this she would keep her accumulated stack of Co-op milk tokens with which she would buy her milk. As a young child I never understood how this system worked and always thought how did my Grandma pay for her milk with toy coins? I was of course used to seeing piles of real money being totted up and counted in my mamma's shop till.

Usually Uncle George would arrive with us to visit and to collect Auntie Alice to take her back home to Knypersley. He would see if 'Ma' (Grandma) wanted any small jobs doing then would set off back home and to deliver Alan and me back to our parents. It was a sad day, I remember (and it heralded the start of the bubble car's demise) when Uncle George pulled up and the plastic domed roof had cracked. There was at least a yard and a half of tape covering the crack to keep the roof intact but it wasn't the same from inside when you looked up and the view of the sky was divided in two by the horrible brown tape. It was after that I think that he changed to Reliant Robins which were a fibreglass three-wheeler like a small van.

Cousin Alan and me outside the shop in Scotia Road, Burslem around 1960, standing behind my dad's Standard 8.

BELOW
Left: Dad and Prince at the shop back door, next to the table where the bottles of pop were stacked, early 1960s.

Right: The same place, joined by my mother. Prince performs his one and only trick.

13. Stories from the Scotia Road Shop

In the 1960s my mother and father, Thelma and Harry Berrisford, ran a small newsagent and grocery corner shop on Scotia Road, Burslem. (The end of terrace house is still there but no longer trading as a shop) Although they moved there whilst I was still at Biddulph Moor County Primary School, I didn't join them completely at first as I continued to live with my grandmother, Mary Doorbar in Park Lane, Knypersley, and from there carry on my schooling at Biddulph Moor. I lived with her during the week and went to school, and joined my mum and dad at weekends at the shop. I did move back with them after passing my 11+, when I then attended Brownhills School for Girls, nearby in Tunstall.

As an older child, I would serve customers in the shop. As a teenager, I would often wander in at evening paper delivery times to cast an interested eye over the delivery lads as they sorted their papers. But as I did get older, and at grammar school, I was often in the back living room completing my homework or practising my piano and singing pieces while my mum and dad got on with running the shop.

It was very hard work for them running the shop because it was a combined grocery and newsagents. They had to be up at 5am each day to 'put up' the papers and magazines - to mark all the street numbers on, for the boys to deliver correctly to each household the papers they had requested. Then there was the early evening daily delivery of Sentinels to go out. Combine this activity too with grocery and fruit and vegetable sales and that was a lot of stock organising and ordering to see to. They also had seasonal stock at Easter and Christmas times which would often be stored in my bedroom, (before sale) when all other storage space was used up.

The shop was open every day from 6 or 6.30 am to 7.30 at night, although on Sundays they only opened in the mornings. The work was relentless. I do know that in the 10 or 11 years they ran the shop, they only had one holiday. There was no one really to take over the running for them. My mamma and Grammy did try to do it for a week one year to give my parents a break, but it was too much for them both and mistakes understandably were made, as they did not know the day to day details of running the business as well as my mum and dad. My mother and dad did get help weekly though in the shape of my mamma and Auntie Alice. My mamma came on Thursdays or Saturdays or both to help out. My Auntie Alice would come on Fridays and help. Surprisingly we had quite a few visitors like cousins or other relatives of my age who would come and play with me.

I missed living with my mamma when I did join my mum and dad in Burslem to go to Brownhills High School. After all, I had gone from being in the country to being now a 'townie.' It was noisier for a start with a busier main road outside the door (good for passing business). I had left all my Biddulph Moor friends to go to a different school completely in another part of the city, so I had to make all new friends at school. My mum and dad worked long hours, so although they were about 'at home', their attention was very much taken up with running a business. My mamma and Auntie Al, however did come on separate days to help my parents out. That freed my dad up to either go to the wholesalers or on general errand duties he had to do.

In the school holidays I remember, I would accompany him to Robinson's, the newspaper and book wholesalers at the top of Waterloo Road in Burslem. Once there it was a treat for me to go around the huge warehouse and choose a book to bring back to read. I often chose a 'Famous Five' book, 'Five Go off to Kirrin Island' is a title I remember, or the complete stories of 'What Katy Did.'

If I was not about, my dad would often take our collie-cross, black and white dog, Prince. I have an amusing image of my dad and Prince going out together. For a start, Prince obviously thought he was human - he had to sit on the front passenger seat next to my dad. He would always sit muzzle facing front and watching the traffic ahead. My dad would turn the corner into the flow of the main road traffic from our shop street and lean to the right. Prince would mirror his movement exactly and lean also to the right, which caused his right ear to flap that way. It seemed that he was checking the traffic too to make sure my dad was driving safely. Put a flat cap on his head and he would have looked like a (peculiar-looking admittedly) old chap going out for the drive as well.

The 1960s were still part of the hey-day of the corner shop because along Scotia Road, in just two terrace rows, there were five shops: three grocery/general stores, a fish and chip shop and a clothing shop in the middle of our terrace row. Nearby in Evans Street there was a fresh oatcake and pikelet business run by Rose and George and their 'Dulux' dog (an Old English sheepdog, Sam.) Despite the competition my mother and dad ran the only newsagent's in the area and they had many regular customers that came into the shop, who were intentionally or unintentionally funny and entertaining.

There was the middle aged auburn-haired lady who came in and insisted on calling my mother Velma (was that even a name before Scooby-Doo arrived on the TV?) instead of Thelma. I think she was corrected by someone, a customer, but still persisted in using her version of Thelma and my mother never said anything to contradict her. There was Mrs Keeling, quite a regular, who lived next door to us and who liked to tell stories of the escapades of her two grandsons 'Park and Maul'. She used to start of in the usual way by saying, 'You'll never guess what our Park and Maul have been up to this week....' As a teenager, if I was within hearing distance of her and behind the counter, I had to suppress a smile over her malapropisms which she never realised she was doing.

Mum and Dad with their friends, Ethel and Arthur Sharman. Ethel and Arthur rented a chalet on the caravan park at Longsdon where our caravan was parked.

STORIES FROM THE SHOP

A great and witty raconteur who used the shop was Mrs Eliza Tunnicliffe. She had a keen eye and a dry wit in her observances about the local neighbourhood and its members, which were very entertaining. She would come into the shop in her cross-over pinafore, (probably in a break from housework duties) fold her arms and start to recount the street's latest stories. I know my mum looked forward to her visits and depending on the busyness of the shop she would stay just to have a natter.

It was not all work though as Saturday evenings were often given over to visiting the local working men's club, which was only over the road on the opposite street corner. If my mum and dad were not too tired by the week's work, they would cross over to the club on Saturday evenings for a game of bingo, a pint of beer and a shandy (in my mother's case) and a listen to the 'club turn'. This was often a local singer or comedian - the club never had any TV acts or 'big' names. It was just a small club. When I got a bit older, at 16, I might go along with them and have my favourite tipple at that time which was a frothy lurid yellow 'snowball', advocaat and lemonade with a cherry on a cocktail stick. Being 16, and having heard the Beatles' music start to become popular, I was often not impressed by the club turns, as they sang dated ballads, not to my musical taste.

I did however enjoy the strip of bingo cards that I played or 'Housey, Housey' as it was called then. The caller made an effort and started off the proceedings with 'eyes down and look out for your numbers, starting with...' Then he would give all their numbers the funny phrases that went along with them such as -'two fat ladies, number 88, all the fours 44, on its own, number 1, two little ducks,22, top of the shop' etc etc. I never remember winning either a line or a full house but it was enjoyable trying.

One of the great perks of living in a newspaper shop as a child and young girl was that I was able to read as many comics as I wanted. When I was younger, I liked the Dandy, Beano, Topper and the Beezer which cost back in the 1960s all of 3d or 4d I think. For educational purposes I read 'Look and Learn', but for sheer enjoyment, I moved on to read Bunty and Judy. Amazingly the Dandy and Beano are still being published today, but the others are no longer on sale. I am not sure when Judy finished but Bunty for girls managed to keep going until 2001. The colour format when I read it, consisted of cartoon stories and print stories of girls at school, girls battling against difficulties, reader's problem page, a few 'how to make' pages and cut-out dolls with assorted clothes outfits were very popular. I believe the 1960s and 1970s were the boom years for the comic industry and certainly because they were so affordable, children had a number of them every week. Of course, living in a newsagents, I could often stroll into the shop, glance through a magazine on the counter and then stroll back into the living room without paying a penny. Great.

Occasionally if a paperboy didn't turn up to deliver his papers I would deliver them. This didn't happen often and I would set off around the couple of local streets, with the paperbag over my shoulder, following the numbers and street name on the tops of each paper. I was OK doing the work and the papers got to the right places. My worst problem was with dogs. Now I'm not the best person around dogs. I'm afraid of them and it's quite true that the creatures sense this. There were three categories of lurking dog I hated.

Firstly, there would be those dogs running loose around some family's garden that growled as soon as you touched the latch on their garden gate in a bid to deliver their paper. I would hover around the gate for some moments summoning up my courage to enter the horrible creature's territory. Then there were the houses where the coast looked clear but as soon as you got in the yard, some dog would come bounding around from the back of the house, whether friendly or not it made no difference to me, I still found them intimidating. The third category was the one where the dog was inside the house, (you inevitably could hear its barking as soon as you entered the yard.) The barking would come from behind the front door as it lay in wait for you to post the newspaper through

the letterbox. Of course, I pushed the paper through the box hurriedly and carelessly in an attempt to keep my fingers clear of the dog's teeth on the other side. This would result in the paper tearing and I'm sure there would be complaints about that. So my parents must have deduced paper delivery was best left to the paperboys - and they were all paperboys. I never remember any papergirls.

Myself and cousin Doreen on the rope swing at the caravan.

Doreen and me visiting Ethel and Arthur at their chalet.

Dad, Mum, Auntie Alice, Uncle George and Prince visiting the caravan on a Sunday afternoon.

14. The Holiday Caravan, from Talacre to Longsdon

It was very hard work for my parents running the shop because it was a combined grocery and newsagents. The working hours every day were long and a half day still on Sunday. Papers went out every day of the year except Christmas Day and New Year's day. The work was relentless. I do know that in the 10 or 11 years they ran the shop, they only had one week's holiday because they could not leave anyone else in charge, as the day to day running of the shop was so complicated.

So my Mamma came up with another cunning plan to give us all a break and me in particular. She had purchased a 5 berth Bluebird caravan in the 1950s which at first was permanently sited in a caravan park in North Wales, near the holiday resort of Rhyl. It was a static caravan not meant to be towed behind a car- I don't think there were many touring caravans around in the 1950s - they were a later development.

The actual site was at Talacre and owned and run by a Mr Mound. Nearby was a monastery we believed because at certain times of the day on the caravan site you could hear bells tolling, mournfully. We never visited it because there was enough for myself and my cousins (who often went to the caravan with me) to do playing on the tree-lined site. There was for a start trees to climb, games to play like 'hide and seek', 'tag and you're on.' There were great double-seated bikes that you could hire and cycle around the roads of the site. We could go to the nearby beach or we could simply run errands to the site shop, getting ice lollies once we were there.

I don't actually remember us going down to the beach or the sea that often but I'm sure we must have done seeing as we were so near to it. I do know that we climbed the trees all the time because on one particular occasion I fell out of the tree and although shaken, but unhurt, I ran back to the caravan in my shock only to slip and fall and bang my head on the metal step which sat outside the caravan door. The blow was so severe that my forehead instantly swelled up like a small bird's egg and I cried even more - double trouble - tree falling and head banging. Butter was rubbed onto the bruise (a remedy of the time) and I lay for an hour or so in the shade of the caravan like a Victorian lady invalid, sipping water and nibbling arrowroot biscuits.

My cousin Doreen and I used to particularly take delight in hiding away from Mr Mound when he drove around the site on a tractor and some trailer device to perform essential toilet emptying duties. Then we would run shrieking and screaming back into the safety of the caravan with my Mamma and announce in disgust that 'Mr Mound was coming round with his muck machine!' We did seem to take delight in our disgust at the arrival of this service, yet of course we could not sully our eyes by watching the 'spectacle'.

When it became more difficult for my mum and dad to get away to Talacre (a good drive away in those days from Stoke-on-Trent, main roads not being what they are now) my Mamma decided that it would be better to bring the caravan nearer to us and park it somewhere in the pleasant countryside which surrounded the Potteries. That way at weekends and in the summer holidays, we would still be able to make good use of it.

I think my mum and dad must have asked locally in Scotia Road if anyone knew of such a site and two customers cum friends of my parents, called Ethel and Arthur Sharman, came up with a site which was located in Longsdon, off the A53 road from Burslem to Leek. They happened to have a small, weekend wooden chalet there which they visited with Ethel's mother to get away from it all. The site was in the middle of the Staffordshire countryside in a field but it was only about 4 or so miles away from the Scotia Road shop and 2 miles from Leek. This was handy because my dad always had to drive any of us there to stay as he was the only driver in the family.

I believe the area is now part of the Deep Hayes Country Park but then separate farmers owned the land.

Once you were at the caravan in Longsdon, you were in the heart of the Moorlands picturesque countryside. The Staffordshire Moorlands countryside does still have a uniqueness of its own. Back in the 1950s and 60s it was characterised by small hedge-enclosed fields of rough meadowland. In the summer these were filled with wild meadow golden buttercups, prim white daisies, clear sky-blue harebells, brown, stumpy chimney sweeps and small wild purple orchids. That does not include of course the cattle and sheep that inhabited the fields as well. The van was sited in a farmer's field in the middle of nowhere with no real amenities to speak of, just a water tap and some bins. (There was a public house nearby, I believe, but we would not visit that.) All essentials that we needed such as food, bedding, fuel, clothing and so on we would take on each visit. Well, of course food would be no problem since my mother and father owned a grocery shop. I do remember that Sunday dinners of cooked meat and vegetables were conjured up by my Mamma and Grammy when myself and cousins were there, on a very small calor gas stove. Nevertheless, they were filling and tasty and nutritious. I remember during the preparation of them, there came noises of despair and exasperation as both grandmothers tried to juggle saucepans and plates on the restricted surfaces in the caravan.

While the industry of food preparation was going on inside the van, myself and Doreen had numerous places to go and things to do in the scruffy, unkempt field. For a start there was a rope swing hanging from one of the huge old trees in the field which we made a lot of use of. There was a small stream at the bottom of the field that we frequently visited with empty jam jars to keep the tiddler fish that we temporarily caught. We could spend hours there on warm, sunny Saturdays or Sundays with our shoes and socks abandoned by the stream edge, wading around carefully over the pebbled stream bed. It was especially nice just to hold your hands under the trickling, refreshing, clear water as it gurgled along at the pace of the current.

There were numerous clumps of bullrushes in the field. Doreen and I would carefully pick armfuls of long lengths of them with their brown flowers still attached at the tops. We would then sit for ages, engulfed in the long grass with them, plaiting them into long braids which we could use as ropes to tie our hands with in the cops and robbers game that we might play. Or less

Prince after an enjoyable runabout in the field at the caravan.

energetically, we could just tie the two ends of the plaited reed together to make bracelets, necklaces or other items of rustic jewellery. If Ethel and Arthur were at their chalet too we would pay short, impromptu visits just to say 'hello' and enjoy sitting down in a 'real' chair for a couple of minutes instead of the caravan's restricted seating.

One particular early, sunny summer's morning when Doreen and I were staying there with Grammy and my Mamma we were woken by a vigorous, rocking motion. Doreen and I immediately let out squeals and shrieks fearing the worst earthquake might be happening. By this time Grammy and Mamma had woken as well (whether by the rocking or squealing, it is difficult to tell.)

Doreen, Mamma and cousin Elaine on the climbing tree.

'What the heck's going on?' my Mamma exclaimed.

'Get up Mare (my gram's nickname for my mamma, Mary) and have a look what's going on through the window'.

Mamma did as she was told by her mother and got up from the double bunk to lift the side of the curtain and peer through it. She stared and looked around for a few moments then laughed heartily. The rest of us looked at one another completely puzzled.

'What is it mamma?' I asked. 'What is it?'

Still laughing, she turned back from the window and said 'you'll never guess.' Aching with curiosity both Doreen and I chorused urgently 'what, what is it?'

'Come and look,' she invited.

We all got up and went over to the small galley window and drew the curtain totally back. A large brown and white face gazed curiously in at us and then licked the window pane with a long, pink tongue. One of the farmer's cows had managed to get inside the small fence which enclosed our caravan off from the field and was scratching its flank heartily against the side of the van. We all laughed. Fancy being scared of a cow! Earthquake what earthquake! We all started laughing again. However within a few moments my Grammy had stopped laughing.

'Oh Mare' she said 'how are we going to get the thing out and back into the field again?' I knew that both my grannies were not partial to big farm animals so this was not an insignificant question. My mamma stopped laughing then and so did Doreen and I.

I took a closer look at the beast through the window assessing its size and desperately trying to think of some means of shooing it back into the field from the van's small enclosed pitch. I looked closer, then starting chortling again. 'What?' the rest of them asked. 'What is it?'

'Look, just look', I said. 'The cow's scratching itself along the side of the caravan but it is still in the field. It's just managed to crush the wire netting in a bit and reach the van side.'

'Thank goodness' were the relieved cries. 'I didn't fancy getting it out of our fencing and back into the field. I'm not that keen on cows.' So we were able to get on with the rest of that sunny, summer's day in peace.

There were times at the caravan when it was teeming down with rain and we were confined to the small space of the van cabin. Meal preparation of course went on as normal. We might be sent out to get more water from the water tap or dispose of rubbish in the bins but during those times Doreen and I would sit colouring and drawing, reading comics and playing board games. Snap was a popular card game with us and a lot of anticipation of the snap would happen. To try and get ahead in the game Doreen and I would quietly hiss 'ssssss' so that we were ready to say snap when two identical cards were turned over. Of course there would be a lot of noisy dispute over who said the word first when a snap happened. If the shouting got out of hand there would come the command of 'play nicely or I'll take them off you' from my mamma - so we would.

If it got dark quite early because of an overcast, rainy day, the gas mantles on the walls had to be lit. The lamps with their frosted glass shades were sited on the sides of the van and always erupted into life when lit with much spitting and hissing like angry cats. The white mantles would gradually turn red as they fired up and then there was the complicated procedure of adjusting the intensity of the flame to just the right glow, so that you got enough light to read by but not too much so that the gas flames scorched the wood-lined ceiling of the van. (If they got too hot as well the shades might split - how these devices ever passed a safety test, I cannot imagine.) The popping and fizzing continued whilst each lamp was lit and the condensation that the lamps gave off was considerable. We had to open the windows often so that a through draft of air would dry up the moisture and blow away the gas smell.

We often had visitors to the caravan. Auntie Alice and Uncle George would come over in an afternoon and have a cup of tea, a piece of cake and a chat with us. Elaine and Christopher, two more young relatives would come and play around the fields and stream.Then we all (except the grannies) would have a wander around the surrounding countryside before coming back to the van for our tea. Tea could often consist of: a tea plate with some lettuce leaves, a few slices of tomato and cucumber and a slice of ham and bread and butter followed by a bowl of tinned fruit with condensed or evaporated milk to pour on it. I particularly liked the effect of condensed milk combining with the juice of tinned strawberries. You could mix it into a lovely pink colour and mop it up with any leftover bread and butter to ensure you didn't waste a drop.

15. Brownhills, Shakespeare and the Snow of 1963

My life in Burslem was taken up with attending Brownhills High School for Girls. I passed the 11+ exam at Biddulph Moor School and in the September of 1962 began my secondary school life. I do remember being sad at leaving Biddulph Moor, I had enjoyed my life there so much. Brownhills was a great contrast to this friendly, intimate country school.

Brownhills High was originally built as a college for girls in 1927 to take 420 students. It was built around a quadrangle in the architectural style of a public school at a huge cost of £43.000. The formal opening of the school in 1929 was performed by the Duchess of Athol.

It was unique in Stoke-on-Trent for its time and was before then called Tunstall High School for Girls. Classes were conducted temporarily in the Victoria Institute while they were waiting for Brownhills to be built. Admissions were by examination for girls only from the age of 10. Parents were compelled to sign an agreement to keep their children at the school for 4 years at a fee of 3 guineas or 5 guineas for non-ratepayers outside Stoke-on-Trent. It was almost a private school.

It later became a girl's grammar school. I attended the school from 1962 to 1969 and the Headmistress was then Miss Price. By the time I attended, it was no longer a private school but it did have a good academic reputation and a prestige about it. My mother had also gone to the school in the days when Dr Bright was the Headmistress. Clever young girls were bussed in from all parts of the Stoke-on-Trent area to it. I know that during my time there, there were about 600+ girls who were on the attendance roll.

There was a Lower and an Upper Sixth form and a strict uniform code that all pupils had to conform to. They had a good record of girls who went on to attend university and teacher training college and each year a handful of very capable

Miss Wilmott, the first headmistress of Brownhills High School for Girls. The second Head was Dr Bright and the Headmistress when I attended the school was Miss Price.

The front aspect of the school in the 1960s. The front field was used for hockey matches in winter and athletics in the summer.
The Headmistress's study is situated to the left of the main central door. The School Office lay to the right of the central door. Behind that door were the immaculately kept black and white tiles- very much a restricted zone.
I remember very well walking up and down this pathway that appears in the picture and then out onto the road back to the Sytch and in the direction of Burslem. I would walk along in that direction before getting back to Scotia Road.

girls academically were asked to try for entry to Oxford or Cambridge. When I got to the Sixth form there was a surprising relaxation in the uniform rules - you could attend in your own clothes. That must have been an immense cultural shift in rules to the serving headmistress and some older staff but looking back it was all in keeping with the spirit of the 'Swinging 60s' and the movement for more individual expression.

Prior to my starting in September 1962, during the summer, my mother had an extensive and formidable uniform list that she had to buy for me. The uniform was only for sale at Naylor's department store in Tunstall or at the other approved outfitters in Middleport. The list not only gave you the clothing items but the quantity to buy too eg. 3 cream blouses, 2 brown gymslips (winter uniform), 3 pairs of brown pants, and so on. There was a summer and winter uniform. Unfortunately I don't have that original list but it was very specific. The school colours were a rich, dark chocolate brown and cream which did look very smart together. There were indoor and outdoor shoes to be used daily. Hats were brown velour or brown berets in the winter months and cream straw boaters in summer. Each headpiece was bound by the brown and cream diagonal band. Brownhills girls were very noticeable about town on their way to and from school so your conduct outside school had to be laudable. (Of course occasionally it was not!)

The school crest on blazers and hatbands and badges was of the tree of knowledge in full fruit. This was encircled by the words 'Brownhills High School for Girls' and the motto of 'I Serve' appeared in a scroll over the trunk of the tree. Our school song was 'Pioneers' which I remember we only ever sang at the annual Speech Day held at the Victoria Hall in Hanley. This was an annual prize and presentation event which celebrated academic success. Girls who had left the school to go on to higher education frequently came back for Prize Day.

To return to my humble beginnings at the school. When I started in September 1962 everything and everyone was new to me. None of my friends from junior school had come to the school with me as with some of the other girls. Not only that but I was living in a different geographical area so I did not see any of my old friends after school either. Things did not augur well for my initial transposition to Brownhills. Not only that but I missed living with my Mamma and the indulgent attention that she had given me.

When I first went to the school the first years were not streamed like the other years - into the A, Alpha and G forms, but took their name from the initial of their form tutor's surname. I was in 1N, Miss Newark's class (she was a maths teacher.) There were about 32 or so of us in there and two other first year forms 1R (Mr Rayson's class, another maths teacher) and another whose name I cannot remember.

Our timetable was full and was run on the 6-day system: each week therefore lessons occurred on different days (just to keep you on your toes.) On the first week, on Monday you had Day 1's lessons; Tuesday you had Day 2's lessons, et cetera. The following week Monday's lessons were those of Day 6. Tuesday you started the week again with Day 1's lessons. Wednesday you had Day 2's lessons and so on. Each week was never therefore exactly the same until you got around to Day 1 falling on the Monday again. It operated on a 6 week cycle. This meant of course, you really had to check what books were in your satchel for each day, you couldn't always rely on Tuesday having 1 hour and 20 minutes of gym.

Each lesson was 40 minutes long and lessons like English, Maths and Science could be two periods put together ie double English, double Maths or double Science. It was a much more complicated system than I had been used to. The formality of the place and its list of rules were formidable.

There was of course no running or raised voices in the school corridors. You could not cross the black and white tiles. This tiled area denoted the whereabouts of the school office and the Headmistress' study so of course it was out of bounds for most of the school population. The irony would arise however when you were moving from one room at one side of the tiles to another room the other side of the tiles. You could not take the obvious short route across the tiles to your next lesson's destination but had to walk all the way around the wooden floored corridors to reach the room.

Uniform had to be worn correctly at all times. Skirts had to touch the floor when you knelt down. (Out of school it was a different story, some girls' waistbands were turned over so many times to give the effect of a 60s miniskirt - they definitely looked like they had spare tyres around their middles.) There was of course no talking in the morning school assembly which started the day with a hymn, prayer and notices for the day.

Architecturally, the school was designed around a large central Assembly Hall. This had two large open quadrangles at either side of it and around these, rooms were built which served as all the classrooms and laboratories. The corridors went around the quadrangles in square routes and in good summer weather the quadrangle doors were opened. Then you could take a short, angular, open-air route to your next classroom. At the back of the Hall were the black and white tiles where the Headmistress's room and the School Office were situated. This area was the holy of holy areas. There was no talking in the area and no crossing the black and white tiles. It always seemed to be a sombre if not serious moment if you were summoned to the black and white tiled area! Often it might be just to sort out a register problem or dinner money payment at the office. However if you were called to the Headmistress's study with no warning of what the interview may be about, it was a heart-stopping moment.

As well as Miss Newark and Mr Rayson, some of my other teachers in the lower years were Miss Mellor for PE, Mr Lownds - Physics, Mr Berg - Biology, Miss Chemster - Chemistry, Miss Askey - French, Mr Perry - Latin, Mr Degg - Art, Miss Brown - Music, Miss Meir - Geography, Mrs Browne for English and Miss Griffiths for Religious Instruction (R.I.).

There was a terrifying term when we first years had the Headmistress Miss Price to teach us Current Affairs. This was terrifying for two reasons: firstly Miss Price was the Headmistress and I was immediately intimidated by her title and formal manner. Secondly she would talk to us about current issues of the day in places like Rhodesia and I understood little of the English politics of the day, let alone world politics, and to be fair to her, had little interest in them. She also, like many of the other teachers, when I first went there, wore her black academic gown. Again with her dark smart suits it made her a formidable person to behold. She certainly seemed like a creature from another planet to me.

The number of subjects and of course complexity of them intensified at Brownhills. I know I found Maths and Science difficult subjects to understand quickly. I seemed to be a natural Arts person with my natural abilities lying with English, music, art and drama. These subjects sparked my imagination. I especially grew to like and admire our English, Speech and Drama teacher, a younger member of staff called Mrs Browne. With her I started to enjoy poetry and play readings and imaginative writing composition. It was still however a great surprise to me when in my second term at the school I was selected by her to be in the school production of Shakespeare's 'The Merchant of Venice.'

This production was peopled with girls from all years of the school so it was quite daunting for me as an 11 year old to be in the company of much older girls including some from the Lower Sixth form. It was also my introduction to Shakespeare.

Linda Hillman and I were the only first years in the production. We were plucked from the first years to be the lowly casket bearers when Portia's various suitors were asked to choose between the gold, silver and base metal caskets and their contents to try and win her hand in marriage. We did not have any lines to

STORIES FROM THE SHOP

A SERIES OF PHOTOGRAPHS FROM THE *THE MERCHANT OF VENICE*.

A Casket Scene- You can detect clearly here that Linda and me, the casket bearers, are made up as blackamoors. Linda is facing the audience.

Casket Scene. Stephano was played by Marie Plant, Balthasar was played by Kirsten Cant and servant was played by Valerie Pope. Bassanio was played by Christine Jobling and myself and Linda Hillman appear as the casket bearers.

The dramatic court room scene in which Shylock is just about to extract
'his pound of flesh' from the merchant Antonio.

The whole production took place on the Central Hall stage in Brownhills.
Linda and myself are valiantly holding the caskets and carrier - I was so concerned with the length of
my tunic at the back. Bassanio was played by Christine Jobling, Portia by Eileen Washington.

The whole cast on stage for the curtain call.

Looking back on the photographs, I'm particularly impressed by the set which was built by some of the Art Department and other staff. The leading characters' costumes were hired from professional companies so were authentically Elizabethan. The commitment of the actresses comes through in all the photographs. I remember being particularly convinced by the 6th former Yvonne Le Rolland who played Shylock, the Jewish money-lender. Her performance was chillingly ruthless in the Courtroom scene with Portia.

say, we just had to appear with the caskets whenever a suitor turned up at Belmont. We nevertheless took our casket-bearing seriously. My only regret in the production (as you will see from the photographs taken at the time) was that I spent all my time on stage with my back to the audience. I also therefore spent my time in the wings making sure that my tunic covered my bottom delicately and fearing that I would tip over the caskets on their carrier as I turned onto the stage for 'The Casket Scene' moments. Linda and I hauled these caskets on three times, as there were three suitors in the play whose mettle and character were tested by Portia in her bid to find a marriageable man.

I remember enjoying the romanticism of Act Three, Scene Three when Bassanio (a friend of Antonio, the merchant of Venice) does make the right casket choice and wins the hand of Portia, a rich heiress. This was just as well as she was later able to help Antonio out eloquently in court, when it came to arguing against the moneylender Shylock who had asked for a ludicrous payment ('a pound of his flesh') in lieu of an unpaid bond.

I can remember during rehearsals in the early evenings, sitting in the school hall in the darkness and watching the older girls act out the scenes on stage and being mesmerised. I didn't understand all the language, I didn't follow all the action in the scenes, I didn't always understand who each character was supposed to be in terms of the plot, however I did understand that I enjoyed the experience and the romance of being part of the production.

It is also remarkable to look back and realise that this performance of the play which ran from Wednesday the 3rd April 1963 to Saturday 6th April 1963 took place during one of the worst winters on record when there was snow on the ground and pavements for at least two months in the north of England in January and February of 1963. It was known in the newspapers as 'The Big Freeze of 1963' and became one of the coldest winters on record in the UK. Heavy snow started on Boxing Day, December 1962 and continued on and off until early March of the following year. On the 29th to 30th December 1962 snow swept in and lay 6 inches in depth in Manchester city centre, 9 inches in Wythenshawe, and about 18 inches at Keele University. In January 1963 the country started to freeze solid with temperatures as low as -16C in places. Freezing fog was a hazard for most of the country. In January 1963 the sea froze for 1 mile (1.6 km) out from the shore at Herne Bay, Kent. In February 1963 more snow came. It was also stormy with winds reaching Force 8. A 36-hour blizzard caused heavy drifting snow in most parts of the country. Drifts

BROWNHILLS HIGH SCHOOL

"THE MERCHANT OF VENICE"

BY WILLIAM SHAKESPEARE

———————

ON

WEDNESDAY	3rd APRIL, 1963
THURSDAY	4th APRIL, 1963
FRIDAY	5th APRIL, 1963
SATURDAY	6th APRIL, 1963

AT 7-15 P.M.

just after bad winter of 62-63 (How did we rehearse?)

The front of the play programme with my recently added notes.
OPPOSITE: Inside the programme with the full cast list.

DRAMATIS PERSONAE

Duke of Venice	Gay Hamrouge
Prince of Morocco	Beverly Humpage
Prince of Arragon	Carolyn Lancaster
Antonio	Jennifer Froggatt
Bassanio	Christine Jobling
Salanio	Susan Pickering
Salarino	Rosemary Brereton
Gratiano	Lynne Rushton
Lorenzo	Patricia Tinsley
Leonardo	Lyn Smart
Shylock	Yvonne Le Rolland
Tubal	Janet Hall
Launcelot Gobbo	Geraldine Nerney
Old Gobbo	Heather Baddeley
Balthasar	Kirsten Cant
Stephano	Marie Plant
Servants	Stephanie Pugh; Sandra Hulmes; Valerie Pope
Casket Bearers	Geraldine Berrisford; Linda Hillman
Gaolers	Ann Jones; Mavis Bowers
Magnificoes	Christine Allsop; Carolyn Lancaster
Portia	Eileen Washington
Nerissa	Jennifer Foreman
Jessica	Susan Bloor

THE SCENES ARE SET IN VENICE AND BELMONT.

THERE WILL BE ONE INTERVAL OF TEN MINUTES.

Produced by MRS. M. BROWN

Stage Managers	—	MR. A. R. WORRALL and MR. K. A. WALKER, assisted by members of the VI Form
Costumes	—	WATTS LTD., Manchester
Wardrobe Mistress	—	MRS E. FLEET, assisted by members of the VI Form
Scenery built by	—	THE CITY WORKSHOP
Décor	—	MR. E. DEGG and MISS C. HUNT, assisted by members of the VI Form
Curtains	—	WATTS AND CORRY, Manchester
Lighting	—	MR. G. PERRY and MR. A. LOWENS
Music arranged by	—	MISS S. R. BROWN
Soloists	—	Tenor Recorder SUSAN PICKERING Vocalist ANNE BASKEYFIELD

reached 20 feet in some areas. Gale force winds howled with wind speeds reaching up to 81 mph.

I did not know all these facts and figures at the time, I just knew in the coal-fired rooms of the time it was difficult to get warm for what was months on end. Meanwhile at Brownhills during this brutally cold winter, we must have started rehearsals for the play after school hours well before the snow had disappeared from the streets and roads. I do remember trudging to school in the dark mornings and dark evenings over icy, frozen pavements, slipping and sliding as I made my way. Some girls who lived further away from school would often walk to the school in the morning because no buses were able to run. Generously they were allowed 'to arrive after registration' as a concession to the 5 mile early morning walk they may have had to undertake! The winter seemed to go on for ever. Each morning I would get up and, in the words of Christina Rosetti, see yet more 'snow on snow' had fallen 'snow on snow. In the bleak midwinter, long ago.'

However the play went on and was a success. No one amazingly went off ill with flu, heavy colds or worse. We performed the play on all four nights to an audience of parents, friends and supporters. I enjoyed the experience so much I went on to be in other school productions and design the costumes in my Lower Sixth year for a performance of Thorton Wilder's ' The Skin of our Teeth' in which I also took the part of the enigmatic Fortune Teller, a part I created using some hybrid eastern European accent!

What is more remarkable to think back on is that this was obviously an all female production of the play in which ordinary schoolgirls of the 1960s memorised very well Shakespeare's complex speeches and verse.

In my first year the friends that I remember making were Gillian Boulton, Margaret Clarke and Janet Lewis - all in my form 1N so we did many of our lessons together. Janet, I remember, got involved with the orchestra and choir like me. However Gillian took a more athletic course and got involved with the Duke of Edinburgh Award schemes. That was a relatively new venture at the time as it was only started in 1956 and was at first for boys only. However in 1957 girls were invited to join the scheme. Margaret excelled at languages and had a keen wit and sense of humour which I shared. Pleasingly I am still in contact with these friends and other ex-Brownhills' girls. We meet up frequently or stay in touch.

16. Christmas, the front bedroom and the Victorian Ghost

My bedroom on Scotia Road was upstairs at the front of the house and was the room directly above the shop itself. It had two sash windows that looked out onto Evans Street (the side road) and onto Scotia Road itself. Scotia Road was quite a busy thoroughfare as it linked (and still does) the two towns of Tunstall and Burslem, so there was a fair amount of traffic noise outside my room and no double glazing then to dampen noise. However I don't remember it preventing me from sleeping at nights. An overactive imagination was usually the cause of that. There was much less car traffic on the roads in the early 1960s than there is now. People used buses and bikes more to get to work. If anyone owned a car it was one which served all the family. It was still the days when a small family would go out altogether for a leisurely Sunday afternoon run in the countryside and could end up at a pleasant countryside pub for a shandy and a packet of crisps.

In the Scotia Road shop our living accommodation consisted of two bedrooms upstairs with an upstairs bathroom which my mother and father had built on. Downstairs we lived in the backroom cum lounge cum dining area with TV, piano, settee and dining table and chairs and dog, Prince. Beyond this was the kitchen and off that a downstairs toilet. (My mother and father had the downstairs toilet also built on, before that there was just an outside lavatory. This still existed but was just used in an emergency and had a coal storage shed next to it.) So our living rooms were not extensive but were the norm for that area and for Stoke-on-Trent itself. The only difference in our home was that our front room was fitted out and used as a retail shop!

My mother and father sold general groceries, newspapers and fresh produce in the shop and also at seasonal times of the year stocked the shelves with seasonal goods:- Easter eggs and hot cross buns; fireworks in boxes or individually in November; Christmas gifts, toys, annuals, chocolates and fancy goods at Christmas time. They stocked a small range of fancy goods normally but this was extended at Christmas in particular. At times therefore when they had bought stock in, it had to be stored in the house or the shed in the backyard before it was ready to go on to the shop shelves or shop windows. In the 1960s there were no home computers with stock spreadsheets on them, illustrating what stock they had or when its sell-by dates were due. All this information was stored in my mother's and father's heads as well as the stock invoice sheets.

My bedroom would become a part storeroom in the run-up to Christmas. I remember the large display sweet bottles being stored full of sweets like pear drops, pineapple chunks, jap desserts, coconut mushrooms and sugared almonds. One night I decided in the privacy of my room that I would sample a few of them (unknown to my mum or dad). I tried an assortment of them, dipping into each jar and grasping a few in my fingers. I must have overdone the sampling because the next day I did not feel very well at all. Today if someone offers me a pear drop or sugared almond I politely have to turn the offer down with a slight sickly feeling rising in my stomach.

According to my mother I was always a fanciful child. When I was little and living in the bungalow on Park Lane I believed that there were wolves under my bed and found it frightening to put my foot down on the floor from out of the bed in case one of the wolves should savage it. At Scotia Road in the middle of the night I often thought that there were mice pattering around under my bed and again I did not like to put my feet down on the floor in case they scampered over them. I also had a kind of 'beat the clock' or 'beat the flush' game which I played if I had to go to the toilet in the middle of the night. After I had flushed it, I had to get back to my room before the flush finished or else something dreadful might happen. It was just a vague dread though, nothing specific! It was like the game of not standing on pavement slab cracks as you were walking over them. You would have bad luck if you did that.

There was a street lamp directly outside my room which kept it illuminated throughout the night as its beams streamed through my thinnish fibre glass curtains. (Those curtains were state of the art for the time in one way as they kept heat in - but unfortunately they did not darken the room very well.) So my room was never pitch black even in the darkest of hours in the darkest of midwinter nights. As I fell off to sleep I could hear the low drone of cars passing by the house but their regular rhythm soothed me to sleep. I might sit at a chair by my window and peer around the edge of the curtain to check out what exciting events went on after dark when I was in bed. Nothing seemed to be happening most nights. It might get a bit rowdier on Friday and Saturday nights when people traditionally went out in the evening to the club or local pub but the rowdiness on the return home then just consisted of good-natured merriment or uninhibited pub singing.

One weekend night however I went to bed as usual and the night did not pass uneventfully. I got up to go to the loo in the middle of the night, crept past my sleeping parents on tiptoe through their room to get to the bathroom. On the way back I decided not to flush the loo and disturb them. This meant I did not have to rush back before the flush finished, so I could walk casually, if on tiptoe. I got back and settled down quickly into my still warm nest of a bed and just happened to glance at my front road window before laying my head on the pillow.

That particular night I had not bothered to close my curtains fully, each curtain was drawn only half way along the glass panes. As I glanced my blood froze, my spine shuddered. I saw a dark figure of a man, clinging on to the panes of my sash window, his feet obviously balanced precariously on the narrow, upstairs window ledge. Instantly, I took in that he was not dressed in contemporary dress but was all in black like a Victorian figure or certainly a historical character and was wearing a black stove-pipe hat and long dark coat. His face was feature-less, but somehow contorted. I could not make out who he was. However I had already seen enough. I closed my eyes and prepared to scream out for my mum and dad but no sound would come from my throat, my limbs seemed paralysed and unable to function. I felt my voice trying to scream but no sound coming out. I was paralysed with fear. I opened my eyes again and he was gone. Did my look of horror scare him off? I lay quietly, coma-like, still unable to move. Still no figure had returned to the outside of my window and gradually my breathing calmed and deepened as I lay there convincing myself that this must have been a nightmare. I mean how could a man have clung on to my window and balanced on a window ledge that was only about 3 inches wide. It wasn't possible. Not only that but how did he get up there in the first place without some scrambling noises to alert my attention!

I must have at last drifted off to sleep with these thoughts going

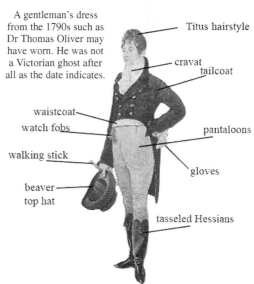

A gentleman's dress from the 1790s such as Dr Thomas Oliver may have worn. He was not a Victorian ghost after all as the date indicates.

Titus hairstyle

cravat

tailcoat

waistcoat

watch fobs

pantaloons

walking stick

gloves

beaver top hat

tasseled Hessians

around my head because I don't think I got up again and woke my mum and dad to tell them what happened. In fact I didn't tell them anything at all about my nightmare because that's what I reasoned that it was once daylight had broken again.

The experience though was very real to me. I am sure I saw a man, dressed from the past silhouetted at my window. Was it a real figure at all or was it a ghost? At the time I preferred to forget the experience but more recently I have read about the ghost of a doctor who is said to haunt Brownhills School. The story surrounding him goes as follows:

A young surgeon Dr Thomas Oliver was taken to the gallows at Stafford Gaol for shooting and killing John Wood of Brownhills in 1797. Thomas Oliver was a well-liked Burslem doctor, of a sociable nature and fond of a drink of gin. He was over the moon to be walking out with the daughter of a leading potter. However matters took a turn for the worse when her father, John Wood, put a stop to the affair. A depressed Oliver decided to commit suicide in front of the Wood's at their Brownhills residence but shot and killed Wood instead. A tragic story of young love and parental protectiveness. The ghost of the young doctor is said to haunt Brownhills' school which stands on part of the site of Wood's Brownhills estate. (The estate had formerly been part of the Wedgwood's property.)

A Deputy Head of the school, Sue Wilson recalled a Wood connection back in 1986. 'We decided to put on a play for our Christmas concert called "The Doctor's Undoing". The head Tim Legge and I wrote the words with scenes set in the doctor's surgery, the Hall and gardens, and the Turk's Head, an ancient Burslem pub where Dr Oliver spent much of his time.'

She was asked if she thought that Oliver's ghost still haunts Brownhills.

'Oh yes, we've often had reports of ghost sightings,' smiles Sue. 'But that's all part of the Brownhills' legend, don't you think?'

If I am in a fanciful mood I can imagine that the spirit of this tragic young doctor may have followed me home when I was a pupil there and sought my attention by appearing at my window, to keep the story of his unfair treatment alive.

But again, as my mother might say, 'You were always a fanciful child.letting your imagination run away with you.'

And so I was.... and still am, I am glad to say.